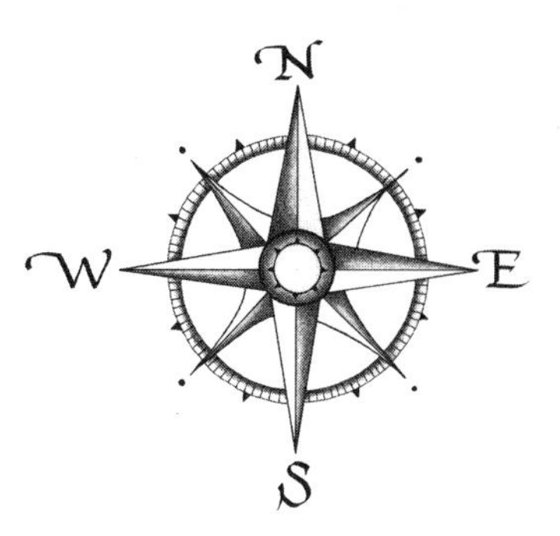

Intimacy & Relationships

Possibilities

for Those who Practice
a 12 Step Way of Life

by ROBERT MICHAEL MCKENDRICK

Published by 12 Step Possibilities
5122 Kylock Road, Mechanicsburg, PA 17055
www.12steppossibilities.com

Printed in the United States of America

Library of Congress Cataloging-in-Publication Data
McKendrick, Robert M.
Intimacy & Relationships: Possibilities for Those Who Practice a 12 Step Way of Life
ISBN: 978-0-692-00324-4

Copy editing by Stephanie Mazur
Cover and book design by Signal Graphics Printing, Mechanicsburg, PA
Illustrations by Sue McKendrick
Photo by Scott Pierson

Into the Abyss dark as a moonless night this place
of secrets and sacred promises where burns the
flames of Passion. I fear it is into these eyes my
heart has fallen when first you looked my way.

– by RMck for SMck

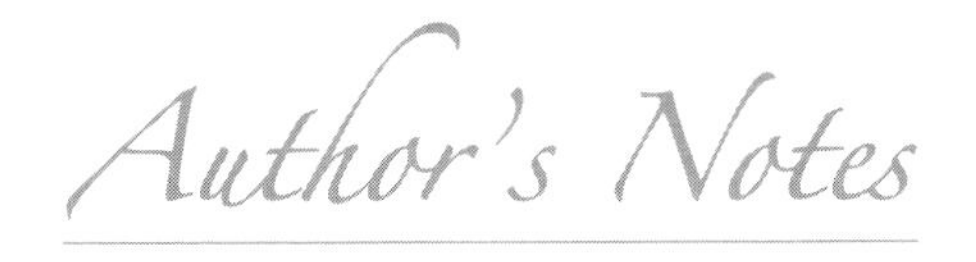

Any income derived from the sale of this book other than the cost associated with its printing and distribution will be used for the benefit of children whose lives have been damaged by the Disease of Addiction.

I initially intended to write this anonymously; however, it represents no conscience other than my own for which I accept full responsibility.

Several non addicts who read the manuscript suggested I change the title to "Possibilities for Those Who Practice a Spiritual Way of Life" as it would benefit non addicts also. While I hope any reader would benefit from the spiritual principles described in the book, it is first and foremost a book for Addicts written by an Addict.

As the author is optimistic enough that there will be a second printing of this book, he will appreciate any input vis a vis the survey questions *(see Ch. 21)* or your personal story for potential inclusion in the next edition. What we are searching for is to share what works for you.

Visit

www.12steppossibilities.com

for reflections on daily possibilities, workshops, publications and inspirational artwork and gifts.

Any work on intimacy and relationships that does not begin with an acknowledgment of the contributions of the spouse of the author would at best be suspect. Consequently I wish to briefly describe my wife's accomplishments in her own right. She is first and foremost a wife and mother. Sue, while a non-addict has opened her heart and home and has shared her love with so many of us who suffer from the disease of addiction. She worked for 35 years as a social worker at an inner city day care serving always as a teacher and role model. She is an artist extraordinaire; the graphics in this book are her work. Her encouragement, counsel and enthusiasm for this work contributed greatly to its completion. She is my Sweet, Sweet Heart.

To Maggie West – my Administrative Assistant on this project for her skills and humor.

To Deb Stephens for her typing and computer skills.

To Stephanie Mazur for her editing, encouragement, and counsel.

To Julie Bozich, Signal Graphics – Mechanicsburg, Pennsylvania, for her exceptional skill and care in directing me through the technical process of publishing a book and in this endeavor has become a great friend.

To my survey contributors and my proof readers I offer my appreciation and gratitude.

Finally to those who have lived this recovery journey before us and in whose footsteps we travel: Bill W., Doctor Bob, Jimmy K., Father Dan Egan, to my current sponsor, Bob B. and my previous sponsors, now deceased, Hershel "Smokey" Martin and Chuck Skinner.

When you honor me you honor my teachers, these are my heroes and role models.

"All mankind is of one author, and is one volume; when one man dies, one chapter is not torn out of the book, but translated into a better language; and every chapter must be so translated…As therefore the bell that rings to a sermon, calls not upon the preacher only, but upon the congregation to come: so this bell calls us all: but how much more me, who am brought so near the door by this sickness…No man is an island, entire of itself…any man's death diminishes me, because I am involved in mankind; and therefore never send to know for whom the bell tolls; it tolls for thee."

–John Donne

Table of Contents

Introduction

There is no need so powerful, or desire so overwhelming, as that of love and belonging. Throughout history, every culture and nation has sought it, proclaimed it, and defended it. From the Torah, to the Bible, to the Koran, to Shakespeare, it prevails through the history of literature. Countries have gone to war over it—such as with Ulysses and Helen of Troy—and people have died for it—such as in Romeo and Juliet. Love and belonging remain no less important today for addicts seeking recovery from the disease of addiction.

However, the premature pursuit of this most human and basic need has caused many addicts to relapse. In times of crisis, such as in a break-up, desperation and emotional pain can either cause us to relapse or push us into the practice of spiritual principles. Practice of these principles creates the pathways to intimacy with our sponsors and our recovery community. These principles also often lay the groundwork for future success in personal intimacy and relationship. Much as the personal responsibility for one's recovery rests with the addict, the success of intimacy and relationship resides with the participants in the relationship.

While spiritual principles are universal, the twelve steps offer a practicality of application that many addicts have found unparalleled. Their simplicity and value in helping change lives for the better has been evidenced in the experience of many addicts who have gone on to become meaningful and productive members of society. What is sometimes overlooked, however, is that the spiritual principles found in the twelve traditions have just as profound an effect on helping addicts establish lasting and loving relationships as the steps have had in helping them change themselves. This book will cover the developmental tasks necessary for establishing healthy relationships. It will inspire readers with the possibilities that the twelve steps and the twelve traditions offer through the use of rituals, communication skills, specific tasks, anecdotes, humor, and experience. We have included the personal experiences of couples who have been practicing these principles in their own relationships in the hope that their experience will help you increase your own capacity to love.

In twelve step fellowships one of the first pieces of advice or direction the newcomer receives is to not become involved in a relationship for the first year of recovery. Perhaps a better bit of advice for those new in the recovery process is to get a list of names and phone numbers of people of the same sex. These individuals will be available to you for advice and support regardless of the success of your early-recovery trials and errors. Most meetings offer a meeting list with a place on the back to write phone numbers. We suggest that you find and use this tool.

In the early days of one of these deep, hot, loving, meaningful relationships, the lovers may not find it essential to attend meetings, nor may they find it important during this time to discuss their relationship with their sponsor (for sponsors really never seem to understand how good the relationship is). But however meaningful these relationships initially appear to be, they are most often of short duration. This is when that list of phone numbers and sponsors become eminently important. The people who you reach out to will help you maintain your recovery while enduring the emotional pain and overwhelming feelings of loss and rejection that accompany the ending of the relationship. There are also some tests that are offered to establish readiness for a relationship. One of the more humorous is the suggestion that an addict buy a plant. If after one year the

plant is still alive they should then buy a puppy. At the end of two years if both the puppy and plant are alive and well this may be considered an indication of readiness for a relationship.

The disease of addiction is by its very nature one of isolation and loneliness. It is generational, often violent, and grief-ridden. Children born into this environment are especially vulnerable to using drugs as both a way of life and as a mechanism for coping with its trials. Their role models for relationships (such as parents, guardians, siblings, etc.) often use emotional as well as physical intimidation, shame, blame, guilt, or the withholding of affection in order to establish control while still living in an active addiction. All too often these behaviors are hidden behind a veil of secrecy and drain the relationship of its energy and capacity to love. The identification of addiction as a disease, and the ensuing treatment that occurs with this realization, offers addicts new hope in being able to break this cycle.

While not all drug-addicted families are like this, it seems to be a common theme. The disease of addiction does not discriminate by culture, sexuality, age, race, religion, and so forth; its devastation is universal. The process of decision making in such families is often chaotic and poorly thought out—resulting in imprisonment, institutionalization, and premature death.

Healthy and loving relationships, on the other hand, are produced in environments that offer safety and promote growth. When we speak of safety we mean physical, intellectual, emotional, and spiritual safety. For people raised in families where violence is the norm, it becomes commonplace to strike out in anger. In healthy relationships though, this cannot be tolerated. Physical acting-out is not only destructive, it leads relationships to failure. If this is an issue for you, it is an area where we suggest you seek professional help, such as anger management, therapy, etc.

In the absence of physical violence, we create an environment free of fear and the hyper-vigilance that leads us to react rather than to act. Intellectual safety allows for free expression of ideas without the fear of shame or blame that is associated with the feelings of inadequacy or incompleteness. Intellectual freedom does not impose unrealistic expectations on oneself or on others. Emotional safety allows for the expression of all emotions without fear of intimidation or retribution. Spiritual safety allows for a freedom of beliefs, the creation of myths, and a faith in mysteries for which there is no tangible demonstration.

Developmental theorists have compiled volumes of research which demonstrate that the higher levels of human experience, such as love or self-actualization, cannot be achieved without an environment of safety. Individuals must look within themselves to see if there are areas where they may be lacking an internal sense of safety and well-being. If so, these issues may be addressed through working with a sponsor, sharing with others, or through spiritual development. In the recovery process, emotional vulnerability and dependency, coupled with a need for love and belonging, often leave addicts searching for ways to develop and maintain intimacy. Without the skills or resources necessary for success, they are apt to fail.

So often words fail us, interpretations are misunderstood, and meanings lost. This book teaches us to develop rituals. Rituals are actions that bring us into the present and help us to focus on the issue at hand. These are the behaviors that can unite us when words fail. They may be as simple as sharing a cup of coffee in silence or holding hands, or they may be as personal and as complex as you wish to make them. Rituals can help us let go of the past, bring us together, affirm our commitments, define our relationships, and help us find peace in the eye of the storm.

We present communication skills that will help us understand as well as be understood, to not only hear, but to find meaning in what we hear, to speak softly, gently, and powerfully. We present tasks that strengthen the individual and the relationship. We share anecdotes and humor because we have found that they bridge differences, dispel anger, and bring us closer together. We ascribe to the old adage, "A kind word turneth away wrath." We offer you possibilities for expressing and validating each other's feelings. Through a series of biographies, we share with you the hope and experiences of other couples who have found the joy of recovery and the love of living a shared life.

While this writing provides you with some resources, it should be viewed as a menu—not as the meal itself. We have attempted to present this material in a non-clinical, conversational fashion. While we hope to inspire you with the possibilities and the joys that recovery offers, it is our hope that the behaviors described in the following pages will better help couples to love one another. It is a further goal of this work to help individual addicts develop strong, healthy, loving relationships that end the cycle of addiction so destructive in families.

Sincerely,
Bob McKendrick

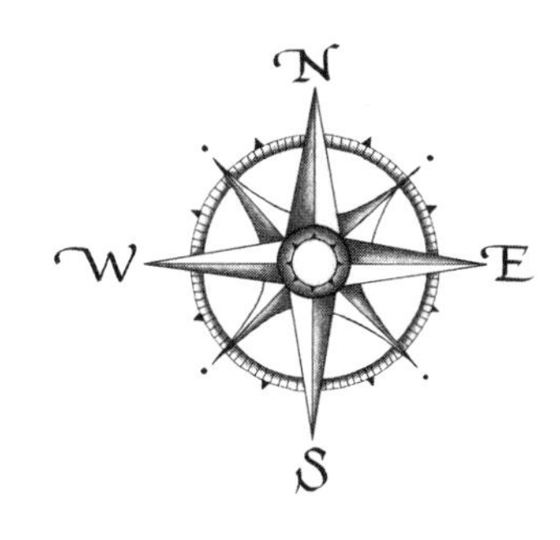

Chapter 1
An Essay on Living a Shared Life

"Compromise is the ability to relinquish everything
that is non-essential to one's position."
–Lyndon B. Johnson

It is appropriate to begin with the recognition that the partners entering into a relationship should be living their lives with integrity; what we see is what we should get. While we all want to put our best foot forward in new relationships, the key is to maintain integrity while presenting an honest representation of ourselves. How much information we share with each other about our past is a matter of personal discretion. There is a fine line between the need to know and the need to confess. It is crucial to understand whether it would hurt those involved or not; discretion is the better part of valor.

The give and take required in relationships requires compromise. It is important to know what is truly essential to us as individuals. In its truest sense, compromise is not relinquishing anything. Compromise is working through a situation until a commonly acceptable solution is found. It is not capitulation—it is accepting and honoring the perception of others.

One cannot get to a new destination without leaving the old one. Yet some addicts try to enter relationships while still practicing behaviors that contra indicate their good intentions. There is little hope of creating a meaningful and lasting relationship while still holding onto an old one. This is often done for emotional or financial benefit. Addicts who behave in this manner eventually ask themselves why they haven't developed the ability to cultivate loving and lasting relationships. For many of us it is apparent what the correct thing to do is, but what we often lack is the strength to do it. Addicts who have felt the powerlessness of their addiction know that they can count on a higher power to provide the strength necessary to change their lives.

Our second step in recovery is the process of coming to believe. It is the time when we define for ourselves, through the process of recovery, what beliefs will afford us freedom and the ability to live a new life with integrity. This step teaches us the power of truth, especially within ourselves. Truth provides us with the basis for a relationship. It allows us to present ourselves to another human being without the fear of inadequacy often associated with the disease of addiction. It teaches us not to place our sense of well being or safety into the hands of another person, but to continue to maintain personal responsibility. While maintaining personal responsibility we may still seek help outside ourselves. This help may be a sponsor, support network, or a twelve step fellowship. It could include seeking professional help or acquiring a spiritual director. Through prayer and meditation we develop an awakening of spirit that strengthens our ability to live from an internal set of values. In the spirit of self-acceptance we learn to accept others. This allows us to honor another human being by valuing them.

I had a friend who was living in a retirement community. I asked her one day where she would like to have lunch, and she named a restaurant. I asked when we were leaving the residence if that's still where she wanted to eat. She said that no, she wanted to go to another restaurant. At which point I said "Well it looks like you're exercising your prerogative to change your mind." "Yes Bob," she replied, "a wise person always allows themselves the opportunity to change their mind—Fools never do."

The second step provides us with the strength to be flexible while accepting life on life's terms. It is a skill much needed in developing a shared life. For many of us, developing a reliance on a higher power establishes a consistently reliable source of strength, an ability to trust, and a resource that allows us to love freely without expectation of anything in return, and more importantly to love in spite of the risk of failure.

The second tradition teaches us that the ultimate authority in our relationship is a loving God. While some people in recovery believe they have the right to define God, this tradition tells us that any God must be loving. The act of believing allows us to establish common ground with which to communicate. It allows us to define the principals on which our relationship exists. It guides us in a practical sense to find our collective conscience and pursue our common welfare. How one hears God in a relationship may be through continuing conversation until a resolution acceptable to both parties is found. Sometimes it may require individual prayer and meditation or praying together. Sometimes God is found in the stillness of a shared sunrise or sunset.

It might be appropriate at this time to share a story about a Shaman who teaches some of his students about perception. Shamans are revered individuals within a community—for they seem to possess an ability to find resolution to a crisis when in this reality none is apparent. These individuals have visions and go into trances, all to benefit the community in which they live and serve.

Three young people once approached the Shaman in their small village about teaching them the ways of the spirit. The Shaman agreed to do this, but suggested that before they began, each of the young people spend a night on the mountain alone and come to him in the morning. Upon their return, he explained, he would begin to teach them. Each agreed to do this.

They climbed the mountain together, found their separate way, proceeded to spend the night, and returned to the Shaman. The Shaman then asked the first student what he experienced. He shared that his time on the mountain was the most awesome, spiritual experience he ever had. He felt lifted up by the mountain, saw the stars shining as hope, and was engulfed with the beauty of the night. He knew that he had made the right decision in seeking the Shaman to teach him. The Shaman replied with a nod.

The Shaman next turned to the second student and asked what he experienced. He replied that it was terrible. It was the most fearful experience he had ever had. He said, "Every time the clouds blocked the light, and darkness fell, I waited for something to jump out and consume me! But I knew that if you were to teach me, I had to overcome this fear, so I stayed until the morning in spite of my anxiety." The Shaman nodded.

The Shaman then turned to the last and asked what he experienced. He replied that he had experienced nothing like the other two. He had taken a direction to spend the night on mountain, and that it had passed without any particular events occurring or any great emotional experience. He stayed only because he realized that in order to learn he must take direction. The Shaman nodded again and said the following: "Each of you had a different experience and a different perception, yet it was the same mountain and the same night. In coming together you have the opportunity to expand the possibilities of what both the night and the mountain have to offer."

Isn't that a wonderful lesson? Can you imagine what great lovers and friends and parents and teachers and partners in life we could be if we honored and sought to understand each other's perceptions? Can you imagine trying to tell the first person that it was not an awesome experience, or the second that it was not fearful, or the third that he should have experienced it in another way? So often we are caught trying to alter the perceptions of others rather than acknowledge their own truth and experience. In relationships we all bring different perceptions of life based on upbringing and experiences. This presents couples with the opportunity to enrich relationships rather than to diminish them.

Often in the beginning of new relationships we struggle with the practicality of living together and having it our own way. While we work through the issues of developing a shared life, a gentleness of spirit towards each other and a mutual respect provide the cement that can hold the relationship together. It is best to establish the rituals and methods of communication that are necessary to work though disagreements and crisis before they occur, rather than trying to iron them out while in conflict. These rituals may be as simple as sitting quietly with each other while burning incense and cleansing one's spirit with the smoke that arises from it. Each person could sit quietly and listen to the perception of the other acknowledging what each has heard the other say before beginning to speak their own perception. Another ritual may be sharing a list of positive affirmations about the other and listening to them share their affirmations of you. The key is to use these methods (or others) for calming emotions, allowing reason to prevail, and finding the voice of God in your relationship.

It may benefit some people to have a brief discussion about blending families. Some of us enter into marriage with the responsibility of raising children from a previous relationship. Hopefully the spiritual principles that we derive from our recovery allow us to escape the self-centeredness of our disease and make it possible to fully love all parties who will comprise the family. It is the recognition that personal time will need to be shared. It will require an honest and frank assessment of how each person views parenting. Some have failed because of co-dependent relationships existing between parent and child that go beyond the appropriateness of the child's stage of development. Others have failed because one or more of the individuals in the partnership could not relinquish their need to be the center of all the time and attention.

It may be helpful to note that our children have shared the pains of the disease of addiction and have been exposed to whatever that included. They may, therefore, lack the ability to trust or accept authority. In spite of these issues a desire to love, nurture, and role model appropriate behavior on our part (over time) has allowed many blended families to become a source of great joy.

The beliefs we hold either individually or collectively can strengthen a relationship. For many of us the willingness to believe in our ability to be in loving, long-term relationships and to practice relationship-building skills are not commonly-held ideas. However, if something is worth doing, it is worth doing poorly enough and long enough until one gets good at it. A belief that our relationship will last "'til death do us part" allows us to give up our self-centeredness, overcome the need for instant gratification and relinquish our fear of failure.

Because of the destructive force of the disease of addiction and our ensuing failures in maintaining meaningful relationships, many of us have found it difficult to bond emotionally and spiritually. Often we practice behaviors that self-fulfill this prophecy, believing that we will never be able to be loved or to be loving enough to have a relationship. A belief in the permanence of a relationship allows us to surrender the petty issues that became so important in past relationships and may have even destroyed them. The understanding and tenderness of the parties involved go a long way in healing this aspect of the disease. Each person must come to believe that the other is committed to the relationship and worthy of their trust.

We need to assign value to the relationship and visit those values frequently. We need to practice mutual respect, spend special time together, share resources, and honor commitments. A relationship requires the flexibility necessary to accommodate each individual's logistical needs. It should allow for differences of opinion, and conflict resolution. It is helpful for relationships to have clearly defined boundaries and for the participants in the relationship to believe in its sanctity. It should be mutually fulfilling. We should be able to rely on each other. We should strive to live passionately and with compassion for others. Our relationships can be a resource for people in our extended or recovery family. The security found in successful relationships transcends the boundaries of time and space.

Love allows us to bring forth the eternal child that lives within us. It is the part of us that plays in the garden with a sense of wonder, awe, and freedom. It allows us to act spontaneously, and to be at one with our feelings. It is perhaps also our strongest part, for it allows us to love in the face of the sorrows and the finality that life offers. Love allows us to share our innermost self with another human being. Perhaps the greatest definition of love is found in 1 Corinthians 13:

Love is patient. *Love allows us to accept our own shortcomings and defects of character as well as those of others. It allows time for healing and for growth. It does not seek to elevate itself at the expense of others.*

Love is kind. *It seeks to understand rather than to be understood. It seeks to touch gently rather than to strike in anger. It visits the sick and imprisoned, it feeds the hungry, clothes the naked, give solace to the weary, and provides shelter to the homeless. It opens its home and resources to the community at large.*

Love does not envy, it does not boast, it is not proud. *It does not shame nor does it blame. It seeks to comfort, encourage, uplift, and to educate others. It acknowledges the accomplishments of others. It is not rude; it does not say mean, hateful things that damage one emotionally. It does not put down one's inabilities, but points out one's accomplishments. It is not self-seeking. It finds a way to help others and to answer their needs. It is not easily angered, it does not holler, shout, belittle, or put others down. It keeps no record of wrongs; it gives freely rather than bargains. It carries no resentments and sheds bitterness.*

Love does not delight in evil but rejoices in truth. *It does not talk behind the backs of others. It does not gossip, it does not seek to diminish others with falsehoods or innuendo. It speaks candidly and honestly even in the face of power or feelings of fear.*

It always protects, always trusts, always hopes, and always perseveres. *Love provides a safe environment in which to grow. It believes in possibilities. It encourages dreams and aspirations. It continues to love even when it is painful to do so. For those who have children in the grips of the disease of addiction, long suffering and perseverance are familiar.*

Love never fails. *It defeats adversity and transcends death.*

Living a shared life gives us the opportunity to practice love while developing a history with each other. A shared life is one of life's greatest spiritual experiences. However, like all spiritual principles, it is paradoxical, providing us both joy and sorrow. A relationship's identity is formed by the beliefs and behaviors of the people in it. It requires the surrender of personal choice in order for common welfare to be found. Most of us have found that adding God to the relationship provides a significant dimension to its success.

When individuals in a relationship commit to the concept of relationship, as well as to each other, it allows for a dimension that many find helpful in times of turmoil. For example, if I become angry with you or you with me, and we are committed to each other (rather than a sense of relationship) our humanness can lead us to fail each other. However, if we are committed to a relationship where love exists, that added spiritual dimension never fails us. It allows us the freedom to practice patience, kindness, and tolerance in the belief that the spiritual forces at work in our relationship will bring positive resolution to the issue.

Relationship is not only about work and shared responsibility. It is about romance and quiet time such as sharing coffee or tea on a cold winter night in front of the fire place. Discussing a book, doing projects together and caring for each other in times of illness add emotional depth and strength to the relationship. Successful relationships offer hope in times of hopelessness and kindness even when it is not warranted. The bounds of the relationship are strengthened over time. It is being able to say "Do you remember"? and having your partner say "Yes, I *do.*"

All the colors of the universe are derivatives of three primary colors: red, yellow, and blue. We offer you the analogy that blending you, your partner, and God offers endless opportunities of a life together, much as blending the three primary colors enrich our vision.

The doctor who treated me in the beginning of my recovery and who later became my friend, Dean Olewiler, studied with the Nobel Prize winner Albert Schweitzer. He once asked Schweitzer what he thought was the greatest of the 10 commandments. Schweitzer replied, "There is only one commandment: to love."

In the first step of recovery we learn the principle of surrendering those things over which we are powerless. In a relationship, we quickly learn that we are powerless over our partner. With the acceptance of this, we form the basis for communication and manageability in our lives. Manageability in our own life will help to enable manageability in the relationship. The opportunity to share ideas and responsibilities with one another can be a rewarding experience.

Personal responsibility requires the division of labor. This principle is vital to healthy relationships. Some common examples are paying bills, cooking, cleaning, maintaining one's own recovery, finding recreation time, embracing quiet time for prayer and meditation, and fulfilling our need for intimacy. My sponsor taught me that one of the purest gifts we can give each other is our time. The proper use of time is one of the keys needed for developing manageability. Once given, time is irreplaceable. The act of love requires a giving of time, but manageability requires that we give it wisely. It is a tremendous responsibility we share when working, raising a family, maintaining recovery, and being a productive member of society. It is not uncommon for us to feel stressed and overwhelmed, for there are periods of life where we seem to be peddling our bike as fast as we can and to be going nowhere. One of the things my wife and I have found most helpful is to acknowledge our feelings of stress to each other and then help each other recognize what a good job we are actually doing.

Requirements for a relationship are very similar to those of recovery such as committing with complete abandon, being honest, open minded, and willing. Relationships require us to live in the moment, to let go of the past, and not to project the future. It is in the surrender of our self-centered expectations that we develop the values that strengthen relationships.

Manageability requires an understanding and acceptance of personal responsibility. It lays the foundation for providing our basic needs such as survival (food, shelter, and clothing), love and belonging, the power of choice, and our ability to have fun. It provides both a sense of freedom and commitment. In our first tradition we are taught to find our common welfare. This gives us the ability to see beyond our personal desires to those that strengthen our relationships.

An example of this is sacrificing clothes for yourself in order to provide school clothes for your children. Our first tradition also teaches us to place the value of the relationship above any issue. For addicts who have lived with feelings of failure and inadequacy being right often leads to exhibitions of self-righteousness. I would like to share a story about my personal experience with this.

I had stopped smoking cigarettes in the early part of my recovery, but my wife continued to smoke. It was our daily practice that I would awaken first, put on the coffee, do my daily spiritual readings, and then awaken her to share coffee and quiet time. On one particular morning when I did this, I went into the living room and smelled the stale odors of the cigarette smoke from the prior evening. I decided then and there that she was going to quit smoking.

Having strong communication skills, I began the discussion by saying, "I'd really like to share something with you. I am concerned about your health and the fact that your smoking could lead to lung cancer." It is a common occurrence that my mouth takes on a life of its own. I say things that have not necessarily been well thought out. Such was the case in this situation.

I went on to tell her that when I kissed her I could taste cigarettes on her breath, that she burnt little holes in the furniture, there were dirty ash trays everywhere, and it was like rolling up money and then setting it on fire. I saved my best one for last...I said she set a lousy example for her children and grandchildren. She responded with an expletive followed by "you"!

Having a strong spiritual program, I did not overreact or engage her in argument. I decided to carry the issue to my sponsor. Now, I *could* have carried it to my peer group which would have reinforced the fact I was right, that she was wrong, and contributed to a rat-pack mentality that peers so often provide. However, my sponsor had a sense of objectivity that often persuaded me to talk with him first. Whenever I presented him with matters concerning my wife, he refused to let me speak ill of her. He used to ask me "How can you say mean hateful things about someone you love"? He would then focus me on my own conduct and on what I could do to remedy the situation.

However, on this occasion after I laid out the scenario to him, he said to me "You are right"! (As a sponsee, it doesn't get any better than that!) But his next statement put the first tradition into clear meaning for me. He said, "If you continue to keep that attitude up, however, you're going to be the most right-est, alone-est person that God ever made." I hope this story illustrates for you the value of being together rather than the value of being right.

Achieving manageability in a relationship allows the participants to focus their time and efforts on loving each other

rather trying to manage discord. Many of us carry failures of the past into present relationships. One of the rituals that you may find helpful as a couple is to individually list the issues of the past that caused you pain or shame. Put this list in an envelope, seal it, and give them to each other. Without unsealing them take the envelopes and burn them. Say to each other, "I surrender all the issues in my past in the hopes of a loving future with you."

One of the things my wife and I have found helpful in managing our relationship is time. When people in a relationship are engaged in earning a living, pursuing education, raising a family, and all the while maintaining their individual recoveries, the relationship can be lost in the sea of activity. One of the things we found helpful when we were living such busy lives was to get up early in the morning before any of the children and to block out that specific time for each other. We agreed not to be interrupted by phone calls, etc. We simply shared coffee and discussion. We found it to be the best time to make decisions rather than have discussions at dinner, when both of us were tired, angry, and stressed from the lifestyles we led. This allowed us to give each other the best part of our day.

It was a time when each of us could count on being with the other. It allowed us to acknowledge the importance of having each other in our lives. It was a time to resolve differences of opinion and to acknowledge each other's worth. It also allowed us to individually pursue our careers and fulfill our responsibilities with the knowledge that even if we weren't physically together during that process, we were together in spirit.

One of our greatest areas of difference is how we manage money. While I never fill in the stubs in the checkbook and instead assume I can cover it, my wife is meticulous in entering, balancing, correcting, and knowing with certainty what money is available. Consequently, having a joint checking account doesn't work. We make each other crazy with our differences in money management. The solution to the problem is for my wife to have her own account. She can still take money out of our joint account while managing our finances with a security that her method provides. In the daily course of living we prioritize our spending on necessities and fun. These decisions are made jointly.

Variations in sexual desire are influenced by stress, illness, absence, and require flexibility. Answering the sexual needs of each other when one or the other is not particularly interested is an area that requires negotiation. Both parties in a relationship must learn to communicate their individual sexual needs with the other verbally and non-verbally (which does not include mind-reading).

As ours was a blended family, we developed the strategy of developing mutual respect toward all parties and defining roles. We tried to role model the behavior that we desired in our children. As three of our four children also suffered from the disease of addiction, we were required to set limits and boundaries which were extremely difficult to maintain. We still remained willing to participate in their lives and to help when they were ready to seek recovery.

We divided labor with the understanding that both of us worked outside of the home and both had responsibility to provide the labor necessary for the home to function properly. For example I took care of the outside of the house, cooked meals, and shopped, while my wife paid bills, managed resources, cleaned, and did laundry. The key to successful managing is flexibility, understanding, and communication.

Thoughts

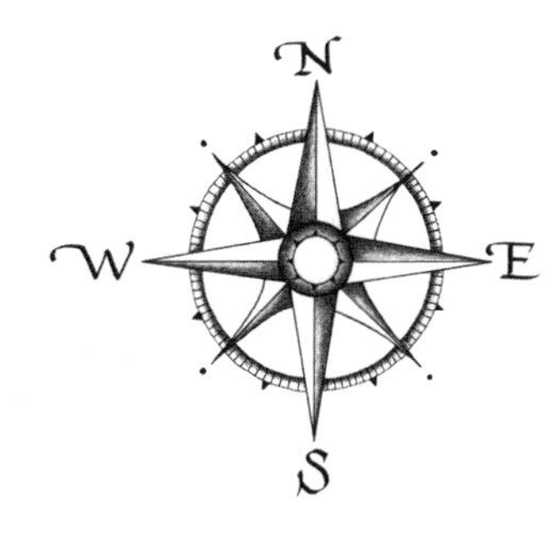

Chapter 2
Sponsorship

"Just for today, I will have faith in someone [in NA] who believes in me and wants to help me in my recovery."
–from Just for Today

The most significant relationship in recovery is that with a sponsor. It can establish the guidelines and create pathways for us to have healthy and lasting relationships with others. In sponsorship we are loved until we can learn to love ourselves. For many of us entering recovery, we were at the lowest points in our lives and often in a state of desperation. A sponsor is someone who will listen to our ramblings, tolerate our self-centeredness, overlook our shortcomings, and teach us a new way to live. By being accepted in a nonjudgmental fashion, we, over time, develop the ability to set aside our denial and become honest with ourselves and others. In learning to take direction from a sponsor, we begin to trust and become trustworthy.

By allowing another person to influence our thinking and

behavior, we become open-minded to accepting direction. This honesty and open-mindedness creates a willingness on our part to develop new attitudes and practice new behaviors. This often brings about manageability and growth in our lives. The principles learned from our sponsors allow us to develop and maintain not only romantic, but platonic relationships. The principles learned through sponsorship also help us establish a support network and provide us with the framework necessary for intimate and committed relationships.

While in the grip of the disease of addiction, many of us used our personal gifts as a commodity to be bought, sold, or traded. Our intent was to get the most while giving the least. These negative behaviors contributed to our inability to trust or to develop healthy relationships. When we sold our bodies and our souls, we surrendered the ability to be honest in either our thinking or our conduct. Consequently, we lost the ability to hope and felt alienated from ourselves and from others.

It was out of desperation that we found the motivation for change. This desperation precipitated our acceptance of powerlessness and the surrender of our self-centeredness. This allowed the door of closed-mindedness to open. It led us to the willingness to change our thinking and improve our behavior. It is often the desperation that one feels in loneliness that provides the motivation for the changes necessary to develop intimacy and establish long-term relationships.

It is in sponsorship that many of us feel for the first time the power of love's ability to change lives. In accepting direction from our sponsor we lose our fear of authority. We become open-minded enough to accept God as the ultimate authority. This open-mindedness allows us to surrender our unhealthy desires. It helps us to establish an understanding of common welfare. It is necessary in building healthy relationships. Open-mindedness is often exhibited through the generosity of our sponsors who give their time and energy for our benefit. It is then that we learn to become generous towards others.

Sponsorship teaches us to be open-minded enough to hear viewpoints different from our own and to accept information that is difficult for us to hear. Through the support provided by a sponsor, we make difficult changes in our lives. We change both our thinking and behavior. We become able to accept and support others in their growth. As we work through the steps with our sponsor, we learn to communicate ideas and to evaluate different and varied approaches to problem-solving. In the gentleness and patience of our sponsor's approach as we work through character defects, we ourselves learn patience, tolerance, and understanding. We learn introspection by allowing our sponsors to help us with our personal inventories. It is this ability to assess ourselves fearlessly and honestly that provides us with the framework for assessing the situations we share with others.

Sponsorship and the Twelve Steps

In working step one with a sponsor we learn that to improve our lives we must first accept life on life's terms. We open ourselves to the possibility that we do not know all there is to know. Change requires us to practice new behaviors—even if we do not fully believe in them. We do this in the hope that new behaviors will give us the fulfillment we seek. What allows us to do this is the desire to have, in our own lives, the blessings we see in the life of our sponsor. It is in the recognition of the values we see in others that we become willing to accept these values in our own lives. In the principles found in the first step, we learn to identify those individuals or couples who, through their behavior, demonstrate the type of intimate and loving relationships we would like to have. It is the ability to seek, accept, and practice the advice and direction we receive from others that make it possible for us to attain the same benefits in our own lives.

In the second step we learn to develop the beliefs that make change possible. We learn to alter our own thinking and behaviors in deference to the beliefs that we learn from people who have achieved intimacy in their own lives. We learn to develop the capacity to open our hearts to the possibilities that we are worthy of being loved and capable of loving others. In this step we learn to become seekers of the principles that promote the values of open-mindedness and initiate the process of maturity and growth. We do this individually and in our relationships with others. We come to accept the principle of reciprocity, which is that we reap that which we sow. In bringing patience, kindness, tolerance, understanding and love to the hearts of others, we bring them into our own heart; by giving the best in ourselves, we bring out the best in others. It is in this step that we decide what kind of person we want to be and establish an understanding of God that allows us to become that person.

In the third step we become aware of how our behaviors affect others. We learn to share with others our process of decision making. We learn to acknowledge and accept the consequences for the decisions we make. We begin to allow ourselves and others the privilege of making mistakes, and we begin to learn from these mistakes without assigning blame or shame to anyone. When we begin to live out the third step we learn to make and keep commitments and to be honest in our conversation. In establishing intimacy, we learn that small acts of kindness produce intimacy much more than grandiose thoughts. In this step we learn to act on our beliefs in a higher power—even when it may appear, in the moment, more advantageous to be manipulative or deceptive.

In working the fourth step we begin to call our lives into question. We learn to ask ourselves if we are being the person that our higher power wants us to be, or who we desire to be. This frees us from the urge to control situations and puts the emphasis on our conduct. In times of uncertainty or conflict it allows us to establish a course of action that is in keeping with being the person God wants us to be in the situation. We can then exhibit the behaviors that express this belief. In asking ourselves if our higher power is satisfied with the condition of our lives, we free ourselves from our own self-centeredness and move towards the will of God. Establishing personal autonomy allows us, in a deep and intimate way, to enter into a relationship while bringing the God of our understanding into it.

It becomes possible for us to be intimate and accepting of others when we learn, in a loving way, to accept our own shortcomings and defects of character. The feeling of acceptance we develop in the fifth step, while disclosing ourselves to another person, allows us the ability to accept the imperfections of others. This sets the stage for us to live with integrity.

In working in our sixth and seventh steps we reinforce the power of God's love in our lives. This carries us through difficult situations, removes our defects of character, and gives us the ability to overcome our shortcomings. What we learn through working these steps provides us with the basis for communicating our character to others in an honest way. This enables us to accept and live with the defects of character that we find in others.

In the eighth and ninth steps we learn how to identify the nature of our wrongs and to become willing to make amends for them. We learn how to put the intellectual concept of forgiveness into practice. We learn in these steps to forgive ourselves and others and to accept forgiveness from others. We also learn to change our perception of situations, from an "either/

or" perspective (either you do this, or I will do that), to practicing forgiveness and love. In practicing the principles in these steps, we learn that changing our own behavior is the only thing necessary in order to change a situation. This practice helps us to relinquish our need for power and control and reestablishes the trust that we acquired in the second step.

The tenth step teaches us the principle of vigilance—to be ever mindful of how our behaviors affect others in our lives. In a relationship we are like the mobile hanging over a child's crib. Touching any part of it affects the whole. Vigilance begins first with looking at ourselves and then at the situation. Vigilance allows us to maintain the purpose of our relationship and to live within its boundaries. It enables us to maintain a safe environment in which all participants learn to grow and to love.

It is in the practice of the eleventh step that we learn the principles of quietness and consciousness. This step allows the emotions derived from an intense situation to fall like rain upon the ground. We seek solitude and the quiet voice of our loving God. We allow others their solitude and privacy of thought. It is in the quietness of an evening fire, in the absence of conversation, that we develop a deep sense of presence and connectedness with one another. Quietness allows us to find God when we are helpless to change the outcome of difficult and painful situations. This quietness allows us to see God in each other when it is difficult to see God in the situation. We often feel the presence of God when we sit silently with a parent or a child who is ill or dying and share in their grief. Quietness allows each person in the relationship to come to acceptance and resolution at their own pace. The practice of consciousness found in the eleventh step allows us to be ever-mindful of the fragility of life and to accept the joys of the moment. The consciousness we find in this step allows us to draw, into the present moment, all acts of kindness from the past. The strength we gain from this act allows us to teach and to help each other. This is when the God in me speaks to the God in you.

In our twelfth step we learn that love requires that we be of service to others. In this step actions speak louder than words. It is where we develop anonymity, a single-mindedness of purpose, and the ability to act together in a loving manner. It produces results that exceed what could have been done individually. It is often epitomized by the saying, "What we cannot do alone we can do together." Working and living thorough twelfth step work provides the opportunity for love to flourish, for us to be identified as a couple where one name is not mentioned without the other, and where our behaviors demonstrate that we love unconditionally.

The Twelve Traditions

In practicing the spiritual principles found in the first tradition we learn what is meant by common welfare and the actions necessary to attain it. We learn that our relationship with each other should be valued above any issue that could destroy it. Common welfare and the mutual feelings of love and belonging are the cornerstones of intimacy in a relationship. They allow us to overcome the feelings of self-righteousness or self-centeredness that destroy so many relationships.

In the second tradition, we learn that the ultimate authority in our lives is a loving God. It is in the spirit of love that we find commonality and the ability to accept differences. We learn to approach each other in the spirit of sharing rather than the authority of giving direction. We seek to serve the needs of everyone in the relationship. We become able to exhibit, in our personal conduct, the behaviors that we like to see in others. We strive to create an environment of humility where all in the environment feel loved and develop the capacity to grow.

In our third tradition, we learn that the decision to seek intimacy and to develop relationships rests in the willingness of the individuals to accept personal responsibility for the relationship. In this tradition, we learn to set aside our individual desires in favor of what God could bring to the relationship. The desire we speak of in the third tradition serves as a basis of loving God and others.

We learn to establish sacredness and bonding in relationships from our fourth tradition. This tradition speaks to the right of each partnership to be autonomous. By accepting responsibility, we are privileged to develop the relationship according to the mutual beliefs held by those in the relationship. Autonomy helps to develop the mutual understanding of a loving God. Autonomy allows those in the relationship to make decisions on the values held within that relationship rather than by external distractions. It is recognition of the voice of a higher power that can be found in both quiet contemplation and conversation.

In the fifth tradition we learn how to establish the purpose of a relationship. We learn to establish boundaries and to live by the decisions that we make. When we act in unity with another we become able to express our love more fully. In the principles of this tradition we learn through unity our actions become more productive and loving than if we were to act individually.

In tradition six, we learn to identify the things in our lives that diminish our capacity to love and instill fear in our relationship. The principles from this tradition strengthen our ability through awareness to love one another. It puts our emphasis on God as the core of our relationship. This tradition allows us to minimize the stress that everyday living brings us. We learn to balance the resources necessary for daily living in a loving and caring way.

In the seventh tradition, we learn that the source of our strength and the ability to provide for our needs comes from our dependence on a higher power. This source of strength allows us, through our own efforts, to provide for our needs within the relationship—be they physical, mental, emotional, or spiritual—rather than to attain them from others outside of the relationship. Accepting resources from others outside of the partnership puts our autonomy at risk. It opens us in an unhealthy way to be influenced by others, no matter how well-intentioned they may be. It directs the focus from our trust in a loving God to a dependence on the generosity of others. It erodes our sense of security and diminishes our self-esteem. This dependence instills the unwanted fear that provokes arguments and causes discord within the partnership.

In our eighth tradition we learn than nobody can fix us but us. We learn that by helping each other and working in unison, we can solve any differences that may arise. This is not to say that we should not seek professional help. This should be done in the spirit of acquiring the knowledge and information necessary for us to understand the changes that need to be made within the relationship, instead of thinking that we can be fixed or that the situation can be changed without the effort necessary from the participants.

Our ninth tradition teaches us that we are not only governed by external laws. We are also governed by an internal spirit that promotes the flexibility needed for everyday living. This attitude helps connect us spiritually to a loving God. We learn to count on each other in moments of infirmity or weakness, knowing that one or the other partner is capable and willing to assume the duties and responsibilities necessary for maintaining the relationship.

Tradition ten helps us escape the drama that is often present in our families of origin. It allows us to deepen our commitment to each other and to maintain our autonomy. This tradition allows us to agree to disagree and to maintain privacy in our discussions without the need to seek public acceptance. It helps us maintain our integrity and confidentiality with each other. It is in this spirit that we deepen our ability to trust.

In our eleventh tradition we learn to monitor our conversations with others. We learn to speak well of each other, to maintain confidences, to share experiences, and to offer hope without being drawn into the unmanageability we see in the lives of others. This tradition allows us to love others who are troubled and who are in conflict. It encourages us to demonstrate, through our actions, our love for each other. It is with a spirit of humility that we learn to share our resources and to direct any recognition derived from our actions towards a loving God who makes them possible.

At the core of all healthy relationships is the principle of anonymity. It diminishes personality in favor of principle. This allows us to feel God's presence at any moment and in any situation. Anonymity allows us to give without seeking recompense. It frees us from having to make judgments on the conduct or character of others and allows us to simply love them. Anonymity surrenders the concept of "I" for that of "we." Anonymity establishes within our spirit the ability to practice the behaviors that show in a practical way our value and concern for others.

Thoughts

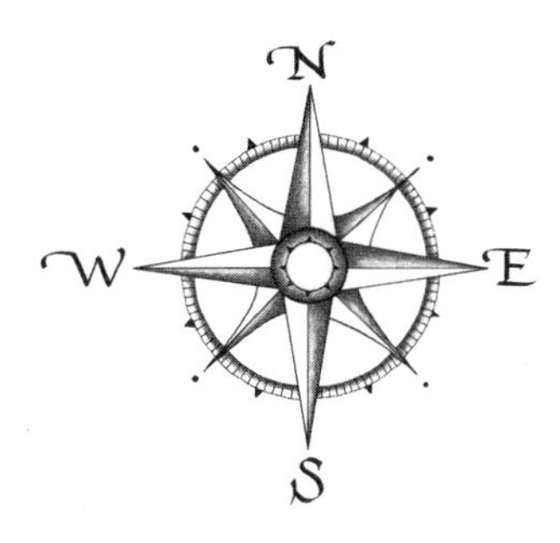

Chapter 3
Breaking the Cycle of Dependency

"From my own being, and from the dependency I find in myself and my ideas, I do, by an act of reason, necessarily infer the existence of a God, and of all created things in the mind of God."
–George Berkley

In the course of human development there are specific tasks that are meant to prepare us for living an intimate and loving shared life. For those affected by the disease of addiction, either within themselves or their families of origin, these tasks often remain undeveloped. Instead, they are superseded or displaced by behaviors designed to help a person survive the addictive experience.

When addicts enter a recovery process, one of the first needs they seek to fulfill is that of love and belonging. While participation in a recovery fellowship can answer these needs to a great degree, it often does not offer the personal intimacy most of us naturally desire. Consequently, we enter intimate relationships that we are not yet developmentally prepared for or mature enough to handle successfully.

One developmental task that prepares us for entering relationships begins with a theoretical letting go of our primary relationship with our parents. Some addicts believe they have already accomplished this task because they either feel that one never existed, or because they achieved a physical separation from their parents at a young age. On closer examination however, we find that these individuals still maintain a dependence on others, such as peers and family to externally fulfill their needs for feelings of happiness and well-being. They do this without ever having developed the methods necessary to internalize a sense of personal well- being.

For some of us, our self-centeredness has prevented us from realizing and completing the tasks for self-sufficiency. As a baby we spent most of our waking hours looking for our parents to care for us. In the course of human development, this dependency is normally severed in adolescence. This event can be referred to as "cutting the apron strings." In times past, most communities had rituals for helping identify the time and methods to complete this task. Unfortunately, in modern life these rituals of separation have become obscure. Adolescence, by its very nature, is a time of developing a sense of self-identity.

For addicts these developmental tasks have often become centered on finding the ways and means to survive or to support an active addiction. In the beginning of the recovery process, addicts often retain the survival skills developed in this process. It is these very survival skills that make the formation of relationships difficult. Such skills are self-centered, ego-driven, and possess the expectation or desire to be cared for at the expense of those around them. They often seek happiness and a sense of well-being by manipulating people, situations, and events outside themselves to answer their basic needs. Consequently, they ride a roller coaster of emotional instability which often creates a cycle of self-obsession. Feeling powerless, grasping for control, failing to sustain their ability to answer their own needs, loneliness, and the reinforced feelings of inadequacy and desperation only contribute to repeating the cycle again and again.

A true breaking away from dependency is moving away from the need to depend on others to answer one's own personal needs. This is what is meant by accepting personal responsibility for one's self. We internalize new values and are able to establish boundaries in our decision-making process. We learn to allow for failure and enhance our ability to learn from it. We become able to recognize and respect the feelings and needs of others. We begin to live from an internal sense of responsibility and direction. Personal growth allows us to answer emotional needs internally rather than constantly seeking validation from others. It affords stability and a predictability of one's behaviors. With these skills we are prepared to live a shared life while being able to maintain our own autonomy. We choose a partner not out of a desperate need, but rather as a desire for mutual fulfillment.

Because trauma is often prevalent in addicted families, it may be helpful to understand some of the impediments to emotional development. If the trauma one experienced significantly impacted one's life, it may precipitate a disorder known as post-traumatic stress disorder. If one experiences unidentified anxiety, nightmares, and an inability to trust or to emotionally bond, one may wish to seek professional evaluation to determine if they have this disorder. A lack of nurturing or parental abandonment often causes lingering feelings of inadequacy. Hence, the thought of separation or independence can often cause an overwhelming sense of anxiety or unresolved feelings of anger. These reactions can be associated with being raised in a chaotic home. This hyper-vigilance has caused many of us to put an overemphasis on the behaviors of others rather than on our own behaviors. Unresolved feelings of anger can mask feelings of depression or the inability to grieve the losses associated with our childhood. Our growth can also be sabotaged by allowing feelings of guilt to hinder our independence.

By exploring ideas and beliefs about your relationship with parents, you may be able to identify any lingering feelings that may hinder your development. A recommended tool for letting go is to develop a ritual. Some rituals include visualizing negative feelings and developing a form of releasing them. This could be accomplished by visualizing balloons and attaching to them the things we wish to release, letting them drift into the air. Other suggestions are writing letters, journaling, or sharing with others the existing impediments to growth. Validating your survival experience may also be accomplished by self-talk or sharing with a sponsor or counselor. These simple practices help to reassure us that we are okay, adequate, and ready to go on with our lives.

You could also make a list of positive attributes and ask others to share the good things they see in you, to affirm that you are on a path to a better life. Building a solid foundation prior to entering a relationship is a necessity. Does your foundation include a recovery support network, professional counseling, families, friends, church, social organization, etc.? To quote my old Irish grandmother, "That which does not kill you makes you stronger." (While this quote has also been attributed to Frederick Nietzsche, I'm sure my grandmother said it first.) The following story illustrates how, in letting go, we become free:

In the beginning of my recovery I had an intense desire to work the steps—not particularly in order to change my own life, but to change the lives of others. My sponsor, however, continued to teach me what a tremendous gift recovery is. When I tried to talk him into teaching me the steps he continually focused me back to understanding the gift of recovery.

Today I realize what a miracle it is just to be clean for one day when you are powerless over the disease of addiction. There have been times in my recovery when this realization was the only thing I could cling to. When money, property, prestige, or relationships failed me, the understanding of this gift was enough to sustain me.

Whether I wore him down or he saw a readiness in me, my sponsor became willing to teach me the first step. He began by asking me this question: "Do you know how you catch monkeys in South America"? I immediately replied, "What does this have to do with the first step"? He repeated the question. I hate more than anything else to not know the answer to something. I have been known to make up answers when I did not know the real truth. I searched the literature of several fellowships seeking the answer to this question. But finally, in the spirit of honesty, I said, "I don't know." He proceeded to tell me this story:

When catching a monkey in South America, the hunter goes into the jungle with a rope and a bottle and a nut. The bottle has a loop on the side of it (much like the gallon jugs of old). The hunter ties the rope through the loop and ties the other end to a tree. He then takes the nut, shows it to the moneys in the trees, and places it in the bottle. He then walks away and the monkeys come. The "lucky monkey" is the one who grabs the bottle, puts his hand into it, and grabs the nut. Unable to remove his closed fist, the hunter simply approaches him without needing to defend himself. Herein is how you catch a monkey in South America.

The bottle is constructed so that he can get his open hand in it to get the nut, which he grabs making a fist. But he cannot remove his hand while clutching the nut. The question becomes, "What does the monkey have to do to be free"? The obvious answer is to let go of the nut. This, however, is an *addict* monkey. He picks up the jar (with the nut in hand) and takes off running until he hits the end of the rope. He will continue to do this until he reaches exhaustion. When the hunter approaches the monkey, it becomes ferocious, lunges, shows its teeth, bites, and makes aggressive sounds. But it *still* will not let go of the nut! Instead the monkey tries to pull both fist and nut out of the small opening of the bottle. When this does not work the monkey starts to sob, cry, whine, and make the most pitiful sounds. He will do everything but let go of the nut. The hunter then walks up, strikes the monkey on the head to alter its level of consciousness, at which time the nut falls out of his hand. The hunter puts the monkey in his sack.

After telling me this, my sponsor looked at me and said, "For your first step I'd like you to tell me what you and the monkey have in common. What are the things that continue to lead you from one failed attempt at recovery or a relationship to another"? In the course of our discussions, he taught me that the hardest thing I had to let go of was what I thought of myself. It is this cycle of self-obsession that has kept many of us trapped in the disease of addiction and made it impossible for us to maintain healthy and loving relationships. I would ask of you, before you continue reading, to take a moment and ask yourself what the things are that have made relationships difficult for you in the past.

Thoughts

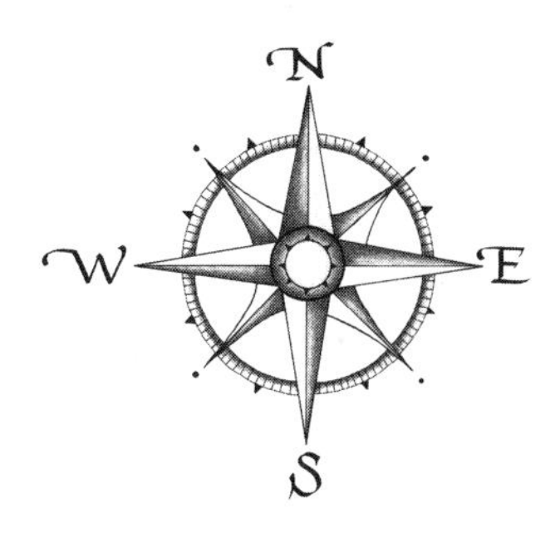

Chapter 4
Preparing for Self-Sufficiency

"The consuming desire of most human beings is to deliberately plant their whole life in the hands of some other person. I would describe this method of searching for happiness as immature. Development of character consists solely in moving toward self-sufficiency."
– Quentin Crisp

Most of us enter recovery with a diminished sense of self-worth. One of the most productive things that we can do is to choose a sponsor who provides cheerleading and constructive criticism. We need a sponsor who helps us realize that through effort, commitment, and created opportunity, dreams do come true. They help us to understand that failure is a part of learning from which much can be gained. It seems appropriate to mention the motto of the Special Olympics, "Let me win, and if I cannot win, let me be valiant in the attempt."

The journey to success for most of us has not been a straight line. Many addicts have found that education has been their way to upward mobility and an improved quality of life. Some of us have come from backgrounds where this was not an inherent family value. The need for self-sufficiency is predicated upon our ability to let go of the expectation to be cared for *by* others and the development of skills that allow us to care *for* others.

Spiritual development places a value on character development and contributes to our sense of well-being. It allows us to live in reality while providing for the needs of ourselves and others. Success often depends on working hard and applying the skills and qualities we possess while managing our shortcomings. It is appropriate to ask ourselves what gift we would like to bring to the world. Here is a story that illustrates a helpful approach to choosing a vocation:

Once there was a rabbit that played with his other animal friends in the forest. Through the forest was a path from which they would watch the children of the neighborhood going to school. In the course of discussion with the other animals, the rabbit and his friends decided to ask their parents to create a school for them. Their parents lovingly agreed to do so.

On the first day of school the teacher decided to teach the skill of running. The rabbit excelled! He went home thrilled with his accomplishments and his parents were proud. The next day the students were taught how to swim. All of the animals went to the local pool where, upon jumping in, the rabbit had a near death experience. His arms were too weak to keep his head above water. Frightened and unable to swim, the rabbit felt less valuable than his friends, the duck and the frog, who swam quite easily. Feelings of inadequacy prevailed over the rabbit and he dreaded the next swimming lesson.

The swimming teacher offered him extra help and suggested he come to the pool after school—which he did. Jumping in the pool, he continued to have the same near-drowning experience! The teacher lambasted him with his unwillingness to learn in spite of all the added help and support that he was given. After serving detention for his lack of effort and poor attitude, a note was sent home to the parents who consequently shamed the rabbit by reminding him what it was costing them for him to have the privilege of attending this school and all the sacrifices they made for him.

The rabbit went to the school the next day depressed. The guidance counselor identified his negative feelings and negative self-concept and agreed to speak with his teacher about giving him a final chance to pass swimming. Again, the rabbit could barely keep his head above water! He flailed his arms in the air, gulping water as he tried to shout for help. After finally making it out of the pool, he was sent home despondent about his incompetence in the water.

The rabbit quickly came to hate school and sought friends who had similar negative feelings towards school. He eventually resorted to medications and drugs to compensate for his feelings of inadequacy and lack of belonging with his old friends. These behaviors led to arrest, incarcerations, and a life-cycle of continued institutionalization.

Can you imagine if, instead of trying to teach that rabbit to swim, we devoted that same amount of energy and encouragement to helping him to do what he did best—run? If the school had contributed the same counseling and resources to teach him to run, rather than to swim, how successful a life he might have had! Perhaps he could have even won a gold medal in the Olympics for his talents in sprinting!

It is important that we ask ourselves, "What is it that I do best"? We must devote our efforts to those areas of our life while managing the ones where we are less talented. Diane Osbon, in her book, *Reflections on the Art of Living: A Joseph Campbell Companion,* shares Joseph's thoughts that while pursuing one's individual bliss may not lead to financial success or social recognition, it will lead in later life to a sense of having lived well.

Thoughts

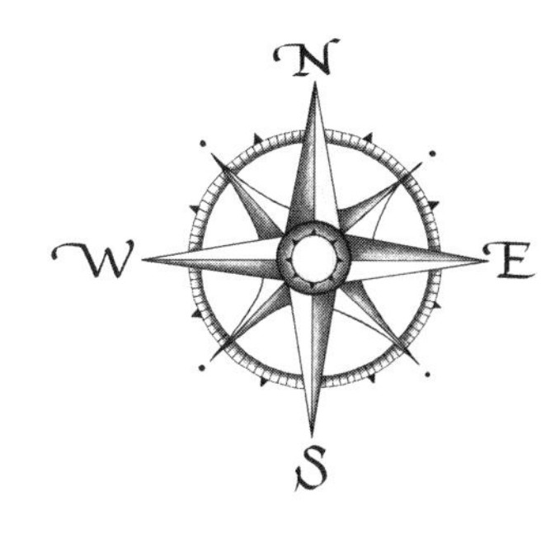

Chapter 5
Building Identity

"Human identity is the most fragile thing that we have
and it's often only found in moments of truth."
–Alan Rudolph

One of the most profound questions I have ever been asked is, "What kind of man do you want to be"? In early recovery I had no clue. Reflections of this kind elude many of us. We often focus on what we want to do, not on who we want to be. So much of our self-identity has been shaped environmentally. Once in the recovery process, we begin to gain an awakening of conscience, and with it, the ability to shape ourselves around the values and boundaries we choose. For some of us this becomes an unending spiritual quest. At the core of our being rests the question, "Where did I come from, where am I going, and who's going with me"?

Life is finite; having a beginning birth and an ending death. Yet at our core there is an awareness of that which is eternal. Perhaps it is in our desire for immortality that we seek to know and name our creator. Mythologies are fraught with creation stories, but for our purpose let us focus on the finite portion: that which we call life. Let us assume that recovery gives us the opportunity to develop and define ourselves in any fashion we choose. What seems a task for many is making peace with oneself. The essence of this is to be okay with our choices. Shame can obscure our ability to choose the way we wish to live by creating an overwhelming sense of worthlessness and inadequacy. It is an issue that must be addressed before healthy self-identity can form.

Many people choose to adopt a set of beliefs, religious or secular, that already have a defined set of values and expected behaviors. There are others who choose to create their own myths and beliefs. The end result should be a set of values and beliefs that afford us peace of mind and serenity. We hope that they will afford us the best experience possible in life. Over time we become an outward manifestation of our internal values and beliefs. The importance of this identification with self is the ability, even in the midst of chaos, to ask, "Am I being the person I want to be"?

While we may not be able to control the situations or others involved, we can always gain control of ourselves. This can be interpreted as accepting life on life's terms. Those individuals who enter into relationships without a sense of self often live in fear, uncertainty, and an overwhelming feeling of inadequacy. This often causes us to drain others emotionally with unwarranted demands for constant reassurance. Healthy people are by and large content with themselves and possess the ability to reassure themselves internally. Fear and uncertainty can push one towards manipulation, intimidation, or other negative behaviors meant to gain control of the situation rather than gain control of ourselves. This behavior diminishes our effort to establish a sense of safety and well-being.

In the process of choosing an identity it may prove helpful to look at others and ask yourself what you admire about them. As you create a list of attributes, ask yourself what specific behaviors reflect them. You may wish to ask those who demonstrate these attributes how they became so patient, kind, thoughtful, etc. Do not be surprised if these traits were acquired through the process of overcoming personal adversity.

Another valuable source for identifying individuals who display character traits you admire is literary or religious personalities. Completing a list of admired character traits will provide a basic understanding of what it is you value internally and specific behaviors you can imitate in your daily life. Discussing this list with sponsors, friends, family, co-workers, clergy, etc. will help you expand the possibilities of self-development and create a path to growth and maturity. Another suggestion which may appeal to the more artistically or visually-oriented is to draw or paint a representation of one's inner self on a blank sheet of paper and meditate on its meaning.

These rituals are merely offered as suggestions. There are many paths to self-awareness and personal growth.

Developing a relationship history with a spouse or partner is one of the most rewarding benefits of a shared life: loving and growing together.

Thoughts

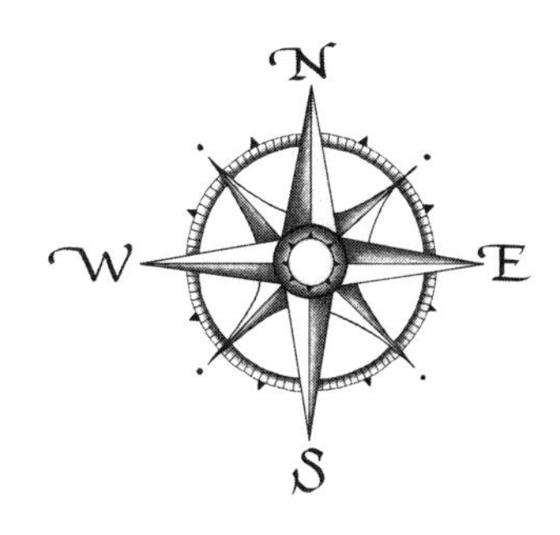

Chapter 6
Establishing Values

"The heart of man is made to reconcile the
most glaring contradictions."
–David Hume

In order for couples to honor their commitments to each other and develop intimacy, they need to each have a strong personal value system and an ability to understand that of the other. Partners must be able to find common ground in their differences and establish the boundaries necessary for trust. The word for value is derived from the Latin noun *valare,* meaning strength.

Values become the basis by which couples make decisions. They must be able to choose freely from alternatives, but only after thoughtful consideration of the consequences of each alternative. It involves becoming willing to affirm their choice publicly and a willingness to act on these choices consistently.

The power to choose our attitudes and behaviors is perhaps our greatest gift as humans. It carries with it privilege, but requires responsibility. It is an opportunity to develop a standard by which we call our lives and relationships into question. A value system, like a compass, is a method for finding oneself while in the storms of uncertainty or in times of crisis. A value system requires the question, "Am I, and are we, living in accordance with the principles we value"? Life is a blank canvas on which to paint ourselves and the boundaries of our relationships.

What makes this task difficult for some of us is a lack of appropriate role models and poor past experiences with both family and society such as church, school, institutions, etc. Some of us also suffer from feelings of shame. Some indications of shame are a refusal to express personal beliefs, a tendency to play the victim, to be self-deprecating, and demonstrating the habit of following rather than leading. These behaviors also indicate the lack of an internal source of strength which make it difficult to function in relationships without developing animosity. In recovery, we often hear the expression, "If you want what we have, do what we do." We are taught to seek role models who have and exhibit a strong set of values to which we are attracted. These individuals are often willing to share about their experience in acquiring their own standard of conduct.

A word of caution: It is important for couples to seek role models who believe in relationships and support them—people who not only cohabitate but have a genuine desire to be in a relationship. This is expressed by their treatment of each other. It is not uncommon to find people who stay together out of an unhealthy need for security, sexual fulfillment, or other co-dependent behaviors.

It is the responsibility of the persons in the relationship to maintain their individual commitment to growth and recovery. Couples must also define the type of relationship they wish to have. This can be accomplished by looking at past experiences and identifying the values that shaped the behavior. Ask yourself the following questions:

- "What new perceptions might I be able to develop that would better serve me in the present?
- What changes in values must I accomplish in myself?
- What values do I find important in relationships"?

Thoughts

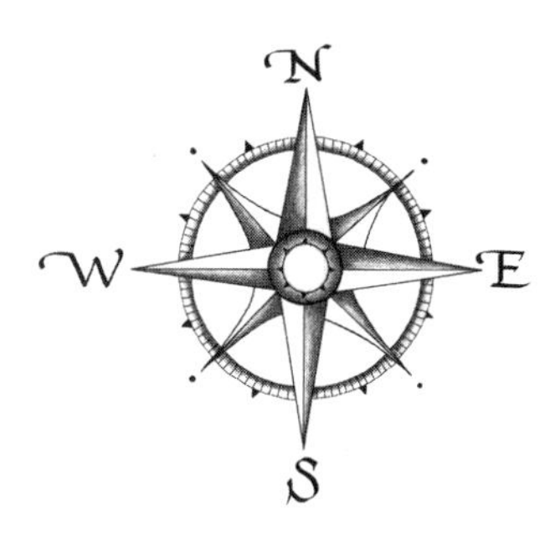

Chapter 7
Developing Decision-Making Skills

"Informed decision-making comes from a long tradition of guessing and then blaming others for inadequate results."
–Scott Adams

Many people entering recovery are faced with developing decision-making skills—a task generally developed in adolescence. It is imperative that a couple constructs a decision-making process that promotes growth and responsible living. It should be practiced repetitively enough that it becomes a natural part of their lives. What makes this task difficult for some of us is that we were raised in an environment where opinions and feelings were never solicited, where power controlled behavior, where decisions and consequences of behavior never led to accountability, where punishment was dealt unfairly, and where teaching values and decision-making were not part of the maturation process.

In an environment where violence and trauma occur frequently, an individual learns to react rather than to reason.

Impulsiveness becomes the norm. These are some of the issues that make it difficult, but not impossible, to learn the skills for responsible decision making. Behaviors learned in institutions and those caused by shame can create barriers to good decision making. When learning decision-making skills it is imperative that one identifies and assesses the strengths and needs of relationships. We must ask ourselves what is really important, what is worth fighting for or about. When is it appropriate for individuals and couples to surrender to win? When is it possible to agree to disagree and still establish common welfare?

It's important that we define the decisions that can have significant life-long or life-ending consequences. Everyone makes poor decisions—we drive too fast, we choose to be late, we eat or drink too much. It is, however, extremely important that we recognize and accept the consequences for those decisions. Paying the price for poor choices can alter future behavior. To paraphrase Abraham Lincoln, "To keep fools from their consequence is to create a world of fools." If we accept responsibility we can grow and improve our decision-making process. If we fail to accept responsibility for our choices and perceive our problems as somebody else's fault, we become trapped in a cycle of repeating the same behaviors and hoping for different results.

For your consideration we offer the following process for making decisions:

1) *Identify* what it is you hope to accomplish or define the problems–who, what, when, how, why.

2) *Brainstorm* as many possibilities and as much information as you can.

3) *Set a course of action*–Put first things first. Define the process, establish parameters, and examine alternatives.

4) *Take action*– Put your plan into action.

5) *Evaluate,* modify, reaffirm, or alter your decision.

6) *Recognize and reward* yourself.

Thoughts

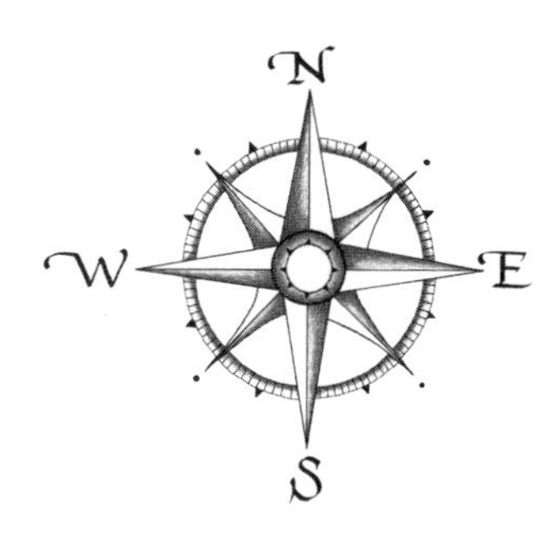

Chapter 8

Enhancing Communication Skills

"Without art, without communicating, we wouldn't live beyond 30 because we'd be so sad and depressed."
–Wayne Coyne

In recovery, our world expands at an accelerated rate. In order to be effective we must be able to adapt to a changing array of new cultural and social situations that require effective communication skills. For some of us this is a difficult task because of a lack of role modeling or exposure to too many new areas of the community in which we must find our place. Some of us lack appropriate social skills and manners. This results in feelings of insecurity, anxiety, and inadequacy. Developing self-confidence and the ability to function comes through practice and direction over a period of time. Once in recovery, many of us surrender our outrageous self-expression in order to become effective communicators. This requires us to be prudent, to use good judgment, and to know how to moderate our behavior to the social norms acceptable in work or educational settings.

Communication skills need to be learned both verbally and nonverbally. When communicating nonverbally, our dress, body language, eye contact, and even an act as simple as a handshake, can convey a significant message. The manner and language used in communication should indicate one's level of learning. Negative remarks or gestures hinder communication.

Effective communication also consists of knowing when to use formal or informal language and understanding how to listen and evaluate different perceptions in the same situation. Open-mindedness requires that we avoid the either/or approach—either you do this or I'll do that. It is being able to process diverse ideas and finding common solutions. One should be able to formulate one's own ideas and simultaneously understand the perceptions of others. One must be able to decide on the best approach and the timing for communicating one's opinion.

Effective communication requires soliciting feedback and understanding. It is the ability to acknowledge others' opinions positively. It is the ability to process new information in such a manner as to enhance the relationship. It is the ability to restate and reaffirm your own opinion in order to facilitate an understanding of other's opinions. It is the ability to end communication in a manner that maintains the relationship and expresses mutual respect.

Thoughts

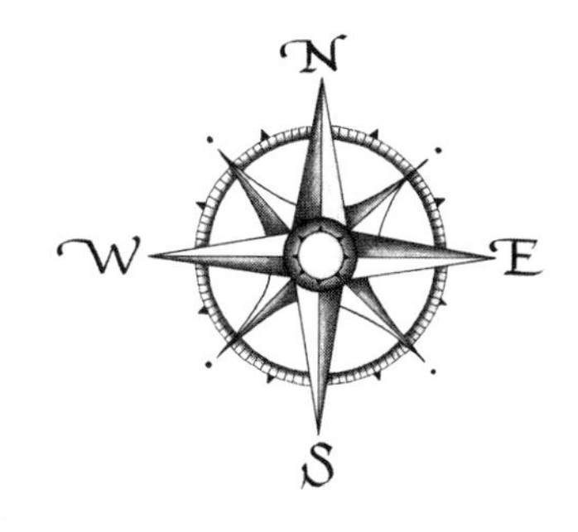

Chapter 9
CONVERSATION

"Let us make a special effort to stop communicating with each other so that we can have some conversation."
–Mark Twain

The art of conversation contributes greatly to what partners think of each other. One of the simplest ways to demonstrate respect is to solicit ideas and opinions from others and to show our respect to those sharing their ideas—especially when they are different from our own. The following are questions that may be helpful in understanding yourself and others.

- Does our partner perceive us as we wish to be perceived?
- Do our past experiences or past environments cause us to speak harshly or with an angry voice? *This is a common practice in dysfunctional families or institutions. The tone of voice with which we speak should reflect our intent.*

- Do we speak quietly and with respect in an effort to promote open-mindedness of dialogue? (Or do we assume an authoritarian role?)

- Do we use derogatory or humiliating language, names, or references?

- Does our conversation convey encouragement and love, or shaming or blaming? *There is an old Indian proverb that says if you want a child to hear something, whisper it to him/her. Another piece of wisdom is that a kind word turns away wrath.*

- Is the character of our relationship one that allows for confidential sharing?

- Does our relationship allow for the exploration of emotionally sensitive issues?

- Do we seek through our conversations to encourage the sharing of information which may cause us emotional distress?

- Do we seek to shut down and close off information we do not want to hear, but need to?

- Do we tend to speak *with* each other or *at* each other?

- When with other people, do we flatter, enhance, or demonstrate the esteem in which we hold our partner?

- Do we communicate dissatisfaction sarcastically and in a manner that prevents a discussion about our feelings of the issue at hand?

- Do we belittle, discount, or dismiss the value of our partner?

- Do we assume the role of a victim in conversations with or about our partner?

- In a public forum, do we negatively share information

about how difficult a task it is to maintain our relationship?

- Do our conversations seek to rob others of their ability to freely express their position by shaming them, by speaking ill of others who maintain the same position they do, by dismissing their position as unworthy to even be considered, or through the use of physical or emotional intimidation?

- Do our conversations demonstrate intellectual integrity and a willingness to change or alter our opinions and beliefs?

- Do we often feign humility as a mask for our feelings of intellectual superiority? True humility is the acknowledgment of our gifts, with the recognition that they come from a loving God.

- Do we refuse to accept encouragement and compliments from others because it challenges our self-concept of being flawed?

- Do we shame our partner by acknowledging their gifts and talents in a manner intended to make the other person feel that he/she is not quite measuring up to our expectations?

- Do we compare our partner to other people or ourselves in such a way as to demean them: (i.e., "You are not as smart, pretty, or as handsome as..."). *This behavior is often rooted in our own shame and insecurity.*

- Do we demonstrate patience and acknowledge the differences in how each of us processes information?

- Do our conversations lead to educating or to putting down the other? If we believe it, do we require others to believe it?

- Have we come to the spiritual recognition that just because we believe something doesn't necessarily make it a universal truth?

- Do we demonstrate our honor of the perceptions of others?

- Do we have the courage to speak directly and with integrity, or do we try to get others to carry the message for us?

- Do we manipulate others into helping shape our partner's thinking?

- Do we gossip and carry tales to sponsors, parents, and so forth?

In the course of my own recovery, I have been approached on numerous occasions by friends, mothers, or girlfriends of addicts who state that they would like me to sponsor their significant other, or they have persuaded their significant other to ask me directly about sponsorship as a way to avoid continual harassment. These individuals who seek my help are erroneously hoping that I can fix their partner when their direct efforts to do so have failed.

Seeking to control others, even for their own good, perpetuates the disease. It does not require the person to be responsible for their own recovery. I choose not to sponsor individuals under these circumstances because any relationship not born of integrity and an honest desire for the relationship is like building a house on sand—it doesn't work.

It might be appropriate to discuss the destructive nature of gossip. Carrying information about others (true and untrue) shows a lack of an honest desire to help the person. Many relationships that could have been salvaged through acceptance and forgiveness have been destroyed because of an issue that was discussed outside of the relationship. Partners may embellish and carry information along the grapevine without consent from the other. Sometimes we place ourselves in a position where it becomes extremely difficult to admit our wrongs and to retract what has already been said or to amend what has already been done.

This can be observed when, in marital conflict, couples separate and one or both feel the need to explain away the reasons for such behavior. One denigrates the other partner in order to validate one's own position and to protect oneself from judgment. Sometimes, when the heat of the argument has dissipated and reason is restored, we can see the situation in the light of a new day. What once seemed to be insurmountable problems now become prospects for reconciliation and improved relationship. But the words previously spoken sometimes entrench us in positions that prove an obstacle for reconciliation. Humility and the desire for reconciliation can help us to overcome these obstacles. In times of conflict or great emotional pain we are sometimes directed to speak about ourselves and our own feelings instead of our perception of our partner's.

My sponsor once shared this piece of wisdom with me: "An argument with your wife is like a pissing contest with a skunk—there is just no win in it. You may urinate further to the left, the right, up, down, your urine might be more yellow, but when the skunk lets loose, there just isn't a win in it for anybody." How many of us have demeaned ourselves or other people out of our pain, which we chose to express through angry words or actions?

There was a period of time in my own marriage when I found it extremely difficult to bond emotionally with my wife because of past experiences. I was quick to express anger in a nasty, verbally abusive way, to compensate for my own feelings of inadequacy. My sponsor gave me the direction, that when I felt like that, to keep my mouth shut and to not speak with my wife until I had spoken with him first. This afforded me the opportunity and the avenue to voice powerful and destructive emotions without damaging my relationship. It allowed me to think reasonably so that I could communicate with my wife in a rational fashion without an emotional tirade.

Without this avenue of emotional release I truly believe that I would have sabotaged and destroyed what has turned out to be a relationship with the love of my life. It is extremely important for us who have grave emotional problems with relationships to seek out a supportive voice of reason to help us work through these issues. It is of great consequence that the person we choose truly believes in our ability to work through our issues and holds the concept of intimate relationships in the highest esteem.

Thoughts

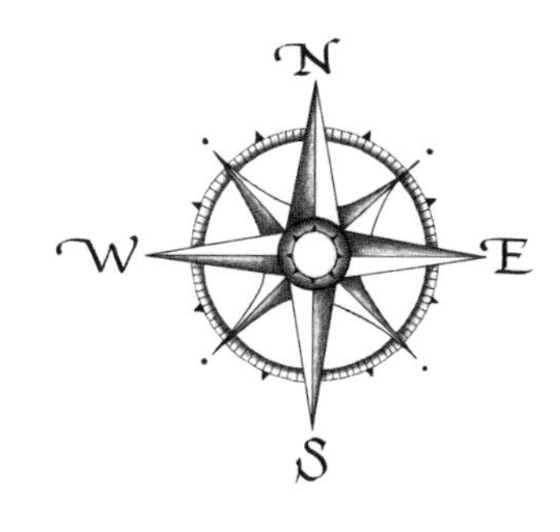

Chapter 10
Independence

"As you go the way of life, you will see a great chasm.
Jump. It's not as wide as you think."
–Native American initiation rite

In establishing our individual identity, we accept that we have changed, solidified our values, and established the boundaries by which we will live. This provides a foundation on which we can build our relationships. For some in recovery it is a time to return to the value structure of our family of origin. We take the best values of our family and let go of the negativity found there. For others, it is the establishment and defense of new personal values which are in conflict with previous family values. It is a refusal to accept the roles our family of origin may have established for us. It is independence. It is exercising our right to choose our relationships and establish our own family's values. It is claiming the right to live our lives by becoming the person we choose to be, while still maintaining a relationship with our families of origin. Independence is accepting our family for who they are without the expectation that they will change.

In recovery, sponsors help us affirm our right to self-determination by helping us process unhealthy family pressure or attempts to sabotage our recovery. They help us demonstrate our newfound values and recovery in such a way as to help us repair relationships and reestablish trust. Some family members may have initially attempted to treat us as though we were still in an active addiction. However, by holding firm to our new roles over time, we will be accepted and valued for the person we have become. It is during this time that we may feel a heightened sense of loneliness and grief for that which has been lost.

Through perseverance we can build an environment that nurtures and supports growth in recovery and in relationships.

Thoughts

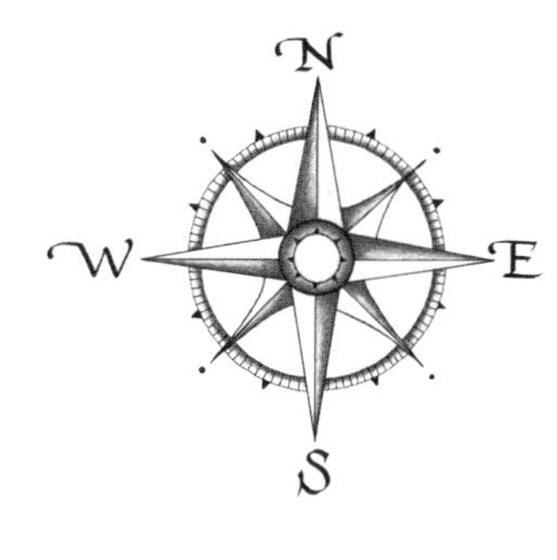

Chapter 11
Sexuality

"I would encourage anybody struggling with their sexuality to go with their heart. If it is not an appropriate time, there will be one later. Never, ever try to rush into anything—do it in your own time."
—Danny Pintauro

Sexuality is such an intimate and personal expression of oneself that we need to be mindful of the rights of personal choice and privacy that are afforded couples entering into such relationships. Personal choice is meant to empower individual couples with the permission to pursue the sexual activities that bring them the most joy. It empowers couples to perform whatever sexual activities bring them the most enjoyment.

The mechanics of sexual expression are limited only by the imagination and physical capabilities of the participants. It is the emotion associated with the cultural *mores* of sexual behavior or prior experiences associated with our sexuality, which generate conflict. It is a basic human right of any individual to choose who, when, how, where, and why they desire to have a sexual experience.

As this is not meant to be a definitive work on sexuality, we will limit our observations to sexual expression within a safe, loving, and mutually satisfactory relationship. Issues of prior sexual abuse or exploitation that affect one's ability to participate fully and willingly should be explored with a professional counselor who specializes in these issues. Counseling can help restore one's ability to choose sexual identity free of past experiences that may have destroyed or limited our self-respect, dignity, or the joy associated with our sexuality.

Intimacy is built on the ability to express and expose one's inner-self. Some individuals have had such devastating ends to prior relationships that they now must ask themselves if they are able and willing to fully commit to a new relationship. Some couples might find it helpful to pray an adaptation of a prayer from AA's preamble. *"We stand at the turning point. God, we commit to each other and to you with complete abandon. We surrender our expectations of each other in the hope that we may find what you will have us to be."*

A mutual understating of unacceptable behavior can determine a couple's ability or willingness to make a long-term commitment. Prior to undertaking a relationship, having a clear understanding of the desires and needs of the individuals, with a willingness to be flexible, can eliminate future problems. Sexual expression need not be limited to just one purpose; rather many options should be discussed. When the apparent purpose for the sexual encounter becomes power or control, anger or manipulation, immediate discussions are called for and solutions need to be worked out. These discussions can be overwhelming and intense. Outside arbitration may be required.

The ever-changing circumstances of life sometimes challenge relationship integrity. We encounter illness, dysfunction, aging, stress, or conflict. These are the times when the strengths of the relationship, apart from sexuality, allow the couple to work through situations and strengthen the bonds of intimacy. Developing rituals for expressing desire can be one of the most enjoyable times during a relationship. They may be as simple as eye contact or the most elaborate of fantasies. Overcoming inhibitions and developing trust can lead to tremendous adventures.

When entering into relationships we are sometimes faced with an ethical dilemma of disclosure. The fear of rejection challenges one's ability to be truthful about sharing issues of health such as STDs, HIV, Hepatitis C, Herpes, etc. Personal integrity allows for the honest expression of sexual preference and helps maintain monogamy. It allows one to discuss and resolve the physical, mental, and emotional issues that may affect the relationship. Here are some questions couples should consider about sexuality in the relationship:

- What is the level of commitment that we each require of this experience?
- Is it a temporary encounter or a commitment to a lasting relationship?
- Is it monogamous?
- Is our relationship a covenant and promise, or a contract with an escape clause?
- Are the expressions of sexual behaviors by those in the relationship compatible with the willingness of each person?
- What within the context of our relationship is our sexual expression meant to convey?

Thoughts

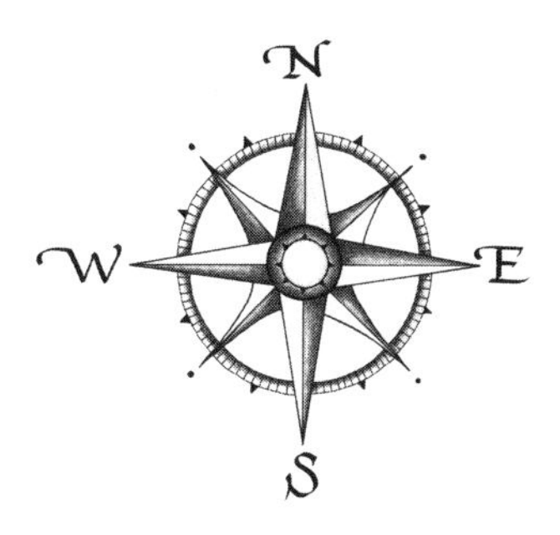

Chapter 12
Developing Character & Establishing Boundaries

"Learning how to control our cravings is the raft that can carry us over the flood to the opposite shore of insight and peace of mind."
–Buddah

Character is often defined as the sum of traits and habits that make up a person's mental and moral being. Relationships also have character. One of the tasks of establishing intimate relationships is a formation of this joint character and setting of boundaries. *Semper Fidelis* is often associated with the United States Marine Corp. It means "always faithful." The cornerstone of relationships lies in the ability of the partners to be faithful to the character and boundaries established by membership in the relationship. This begins with an honest desire to be in a relationship and a willingness to work towards establishing the character and boundaries of that relationship, and once established to live within them.

The demands of living in an active addiction have often created in us the desire for instant gratification. This shapes our thoughts, feelings, and actions. A willingness to change this approach allows us to put effort into the present while waiting for a future return. Patience helps us establish an attitude in relationships where we look to their longevity rather than their ending—where we look for reasons to stay in them rather than reasons to leave them.

Many of us have come from families in which abandonment, either physical or emotional, has been an issue. Some of us have been raised or incarcerated in institutions lacking prosocial values. We suffered the loss of everything we held dear to the disease of addiction, and ultimately became unfaithful and unable to trust. This has led many of us to repeated failures in relationships. While bleak, this past history is not insurmountable. Many of us found that the core to success in long-term relationships rests with our attitude towards God. It is this attitude that allows us to develop relationships with sponsors and peers in recovery and to maintain friendships. It allowed us to complete educational goals and maintain long-term employment. This God-centered approach allows us to develop intimacy and to establish long-term relationships. Faith in a higher power also allows us to accept our own defects of character and those of others. It allows us to persevere through difficulties. It deepens our ability to trust and instills confidence and security in relationships through overcoming difficult situations. Further, a God-centered program of recovery allows us to be true to ourselves and to others. It allows us to overcome distractions and mistakes and to establish a pattern of growth.

Happiness comes in finding pleasure in our relationship. It is the ability to live out the will of our higher power and experience the joy that comes with sharing our life with others. We maintain faithfulness when we think thoughts that strengthen the relationship and honor the individuals in it. It is God-centered values that allow us to forgive and to accept forgiveness.

Faithfulness allows us to speak well of ourselves and of our partner. It seeks to offer words of comfort and encouragement rather than discord or distraction. Faithfulness is best displayed in action. It says, "I am here now, and I will be here tomorrow." These actions of integrity express security and build for the future. Actions demonstrate an adherence to the will of God and a commitment to the marriage.

The topic of the demonstration of faithfulness reminds me of when I went to my sponsor and told him that I had been less than kind to my wife. I was seeking a way to make amends. In my character defects was a tendency to say, "I'm out of here," rather than fight for something that I believed in. It was much easier for me to take flight. My sponsor knew this about me. In discussing my efforts to make amends to my wife, I said that perhaps I should buy her some flowers or chocolate. He suggested that I buy a trash can or curtains for the bathroom. I did not think that this was a very romantic approach to sufficiently make amends. He explained that while the flowers or chocolate may say you are sorry, the trash can and the curtains say that you are going to stay there and that the relationship is permanent. Sometimes we need to focus on the messages that say, "You're important," "I'm willing to fight for you," and, "We can get through anything together."

In faithfulness we seek to love each other as completely as we are loved by God. A relationship should allow all in it to flower. It should provide an atmosphere of growth and maturity and while striving for progress it allows for imperfections in ourselves and in others. Faithfulness avoids jealousy, envy, and the longing for things or relationships that are not healthy.

Sometimes it is better to seek mercy than justice. A humorous account of this is a story about a friend of mine who, while driving in a rural area, exceeded the speed limit. As often happens, a police officer held him accountable for the violation of the law by giving him a ticket. He opted to have a hearing. At the hearing the judge asked the police officer to recount the events of the incident, which he did. He then turned and asked my friend to give his account of the incident. At that point my friend said, "I agree completely with the account of the officer! In fact, I was speeding."

When the judge said, "Well then what is the purpose of this hearing"? my friend replied, "I came to this hearing not to seek justice but to seek mercy. And it is within your prerogative as a judge to grant me mercy." The judge asked my friend how he might do that. My friend said he had no problem paying the fine, but since he used his license everyday to earn a living, he was hoping the judge might offer him mercy by not requiring the points for such an offence to be placed on his driving record.

The police officer, who I am sure, had never heard this approach before, where truth was acknowledged, concurred in the willingness to rewrite the ticket so that accountability could be accomplished by paying a fine, and mercy could be granted by the absence of points.

I offer this as an example of how we all need to maintain accountability and accept required responsibility, while still seeking ways to be merciful and kind. Living together provides us many opportunities to give both mercy and kindness.

Other characteristics of relationships are stability and security. Security in a relationship allows us to think the best of each other, to be each other's biggest cheerleader, and to be each other's most gentle critic. There is a confidence that in times of incapacity, the other person will be there for us. It is the creation of an environment where one can relax and truly be one's self. We can show who we are without pretense when the relationship is stable and secure. This provides private comfort in the face of public scrutiny.

A safe, secure relationship offers encouragement in moments of weakness; it accepts failure and encourages restoration; it provides resources for us when we are incapable of providing for ourselves, such as in times of illness; it is the personification of a loving God who provides unconditional love; it allows us to establish a sense of belonging and to develop a sense of history with each other.

A demonstration of commitment may be the purchase of burial lots together; it says even in death we rest together. This sense of security allows us to make investments today for the fulfillment of future goals. On the topic of death, I used to say that I wanted to die first to avoid the pain of loss and feelings of grief. I have since altered that opinion as a result of discussion with one of my senior mentors. He said that he wanted to live long enough to be able to take care of his wife, to see that she was able to spend her final days with dignity and in his loving embrace. Since this discussion I have come to the same resolution myself. Love truly does allow us to overcome our self-centeredness and to love even in the face of death.

As I approach my own later years, I have taken to asking older men if they have any regrets in life. One of the most moving responses for me was that of an older gentleman who revealed to me that he hadn't spent enough time with his wife, that his profession took all of his time. After the loss of his wife he realized he should have spent more time with her and less with his professional responsibilities. I have used this awareness as a tool for my own time-management.

Another example of commitment and a willingness to care for each other was exhibited by my sponsor when his wife became ill. She required an extended hospitalization before she died. I watched him go to the hospital each day for 15 weeks from 7 a.m. to 11 p.m., and wash her face, give her ice chips, hold her hand and sometimes just sit in silence while she slept.

I used to try to provide him with support by visiting him there. But after an hour or two I couldn't wait to get out of there! The effort seemed over-burdensome. I was amazed at his ability to do that so consistently and so lovingly. It wasn't until many years later when my own wife became ill, and I stayed with her during a hospitalization, that I finally understood how effortless it is to serve somebody that you truly love.

In establishing a mutually supportive character to the relationship, open-mindedness can be displayed by a willingness to share responsibilities while avoiding traditional or gender-specific assignments of tasks. We need to look at the tasks that must be accomplished and then review what skills, nature, and temperament lend themselves to their completion. It begins with a respect for all the tasks that need to be accomplished, whether earning a living or maintaining a home.

Productivity is enhanced when these issues are worked out in mutually acceptable fashion, where both partners are willing to go above and beyond what is required of them. Productivity allows us to establish home ownership, educate our children, be involved in our communities, care for our parents, and act as sponsors for individuals seeking recovery. The efforts of two people acting in unison and moving in a common direction far exceed the measure that one person acting independently could accomplish. A willingness to share responsibility contributes greatly to the ability of the relationship to govern itself and be defined by the actions of the individuals in it rather than to be influenced by those around it.

Humor adds a great deal to the character of relationships. It allows the participants to laugh with each other and share in the humor that life provides. This humor should not be at the expense of each other or of a shaming or belittling nature. It is an acknowledged fact that humor provides healing at both the physical and emotional level. It is in the spirit of fun that we learn to recreate together. Sharing activities helps us set aside the responsibilities and burdens of daily living and to renew ourselves with child-like joy.

The character of a relationship should provide the opportunity for each partner to express their regard for one another in a private fashion. Character should allow quiet time when decisions can be made, free of distractions. One example of this is that my wife and I both had professions which were demanding of our time. We had children in our family and periodically had recovering addicts and foster children living with us. The requirements of the time and energy to complete the tasks of the day often left us with little willingness or energy to communicate in the evening.

In an effort to keep our relationship strong we stumbled upon the idea of getting up two hours earlier in the morning, to not take phone calls or allow other distractions during this time. This gave us private time for our own prayers and meditations and while sharing a cup of coffee it gave us a chance to tell each other about the activities in our lives and provided the time to make decisions. We came to believe that giving the best in the first part of our day to God through prayer and meditation and to each other in conversation allowed us to maintain our intimacy and increased our ability to be productive for others.

The important lesson in this is that there needs to be quiet time set aside for valuing each other and for decision making, which is free from the pressures and distractions of life. Quiet time affords us an opportunity to say to each other that no matter how hectic our lives have become, you are still the most important person in it. It escapes me where I've heard this said, *"Where one puts one's time, that's where one's heart truly rests."* The true character of a relationship and its inherent strength often comes through overcoming conflict and difficulty. The conflicts that arise from our own behavior, be they as simple as not putting the cap on the toothpaste tube or as serious as infidelity, offer us the opportunity to demonstrate our love and commitment to each other. Love never fails.

Finding solutions to problems and developing healthy resolution, while difficult, contributes to our sense of security and strengthens the relationship. Difficulties not of our own making, such as issues of health, have caused many of us to assume the role of caretaker, assuming the responsibilities and tasks that are commonly shared. This has allowed us to serve and to be served without feelings of shame; it exemplifies the honor and dignity that is found in the spirit of love.

Thoughts

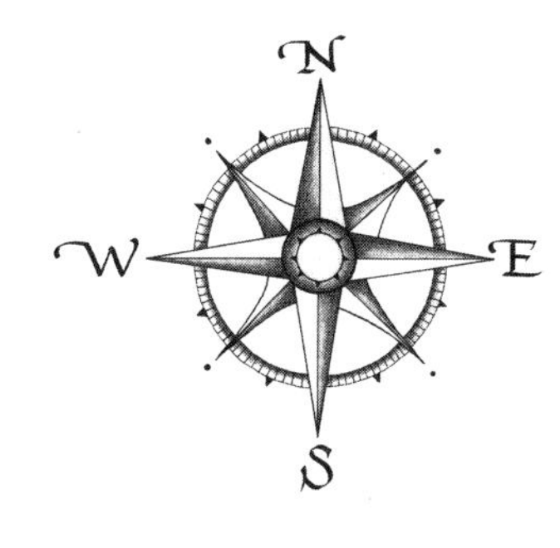

Chapter 13

Autonomy

"It is only the impossible that is possible for God.
He has given over the possible to the mechanics of
matter and the autonomy of his creatures."
–Simone Weil

Autonomy (i.e., personal independence or freedom) recognizes the uniqueness of each relationship and honors the couple's commitment to each other. It shapes the character of the relationship, and helps to define its purpose. Autonomy asks how we want to live with each other and what we hope to accomplish by sharing our lives. It is evidenced by each couple's actions and is defined by the fruits that each action produces. Autonomy enhances each couple's needs for love and belonging. It helps to provide a safe, stable, and loving environment in which to grow. It also provides an opportunity for spiritual, physical, mental, and emotional intimacy. Autonomy allows us to love at the deepest levels and maximizes our ability to be productive members of society. The belief in our capability to have loving relationships is born out of our belief in a higher power and the permission to love.

The disease of addiction has robbed many of us of the ability to value ourselves and others. An acknowledgment of our creator and the gift of recovery is the beginning of self-acceptance. Belief in a higher power allows us to overcome the half-measures associated with doubt. A higher power provides the basis of our understanding that we are loved and capable of showing this love to others. The second step in recovery allows us to define ourselves by our beliefs in a higher power. Our third step gives us the power to practice these beliefs in our daily lives. God allows us to learn from our past mistakes without being buried by them. This is where the principle of hope triumphs over experience. Our willingness allows us to reach a point in our recovery where we can surrender our expectations, accept life on life's terms, and place our trust into the care of God.

In the Alcoholics Anonymous fellowship the surrender of one's self is expressed in their preamble with the saying, "We stood at the turning point and asked for God's care and protection with complete abandon." It is in the abandonment of our desires and the acceptance of God's will that we become truly grateful for who we are and for what we have been given. Gratitude allows us to escape the pain of our desires while experiencing the joy of what God and others freely give to us. There is an old Southern expression that exemplifies this: "You're old enough that your wants shouldn't hurt you."

There is also a verse from 1 Corinthians 13 that says, "When I was a child I thought as a child, I reasoned as a child, I spoke as a child. Now that I am a man, I put away childish things." It is out of these understandings that we put away our self-centeredness in favor of God-centeredness. The sense of love that we receive from a God of our own understanding allows us to develop new values. This belief in God provides us with the essential abilities to enter into lasting relationships.

Healthy relationships provide us with the opportunity to value and love another at the deepest level. Some practical ways that we can show how we value each other in a relationship begin with counting our blessings. We come to recognize first the loving and redemptive powers of a God who has blessed us with the gift of recovery and the opportunity to live a shared life. We have an opportunity on a daily basis to count our blessings and to acknowledge to each other our gratitude for being in each other's lives. God helps us recognize and honor the uniqueness of gifts that each person brings to the relationship. He helps us to accept our imperfections and the imperfections of others. With an honest intent to fulfill God's will He helps us to manage the assets and liabilities of our lives.

Valuing each other allows us to strengthen ourselves by recognizing and sharing with each other our "good points." Valuing someone means acknowledging the little kindnesses that we show each other on a daily basis. It remembers and honors the important events in each other's lives such as birthdays, holidays, etc. It provides us with the opportunity to do the unexpected: to do each other's chores, provide an unexpected gift, send flowers to one's place of employment, give each other cards or letters, or create poems or songs. God helps us to value what the other partner values by giving them what it is they want, and not what we want them to have. Valuing each other is demonstrated by sharing the power in the relationship when we make decisions jointly. This can occur simply by allowing the other to choose a movie or to control the remote for the television.

Another way to achieve a better understanding of your relationship's value is to recognize when the other person is going out of their way to serve you, and in turn, to acknowledge their kindness. One way to recognize the relationship's value is saying "please" and "thank you" and not taking each other for granted. We value each other by recognizing feelings and being willing to work through these feelings with each other. We value each other by backing off and by giving each the time necessary to heal before seeking reconciliation. How we touch each other verbally, emotionally, and physically can be a tremendous way to demonstrate the esteem in which we hold the other person. This may be done just by putting your arm around someone and allowing them to cry on your shoulder, or by holding their hands or by rubbing their back.

Life provides us with many distractions that impede our ability to love. We value each other by taking the time required for the relationship and putting the relationship first. We demonstrate our love for each other by sacrificing our time and energy for the fulfillment of the other. This can be demonstrated simply by watching the kids so one or the other can go to a meeting, or by providing the resources and atmosphere conducive to helping each other reach educational and professional goals.

I encourage you to sit down with your partner and create your own list of ways that you wish to demonstrate your value of or for each other. These are some questions you may wish to ask yourselves:

- What are the major distractions in our lives?
- What is at the core of reoccurring conflicts?
- What causes us to lose focus on our love for each other and the primary purposes of our relationship?
- What are the demands of the relationship that have caused it to become unbalanced?
- What are the things that we pursue, healthy or unhealthy, at the cost of our relationship?

- Is the strength of the relationship weakened by vices such as gambling, excessive spending, or other obsessions or compulsions?
- What are the steps that we can take individually and collectively to enhance our ability to love and to improve our relationship?

Thoughts

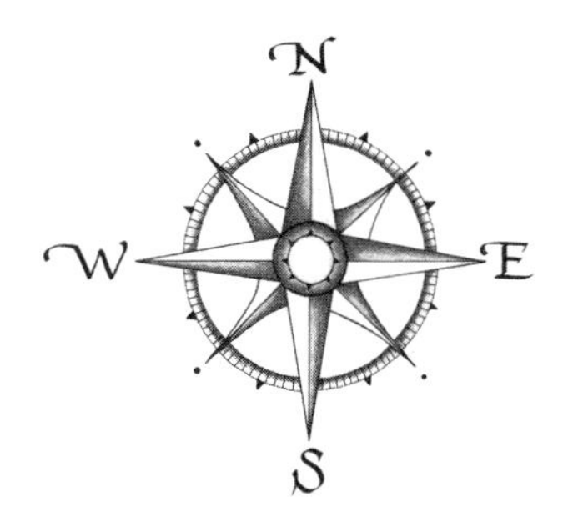

Chapter 14
FORGIVENESS

"It is in forgiving that we are forgiven."
"It is in giving that we receive."
–Saint Francis of Assisi

Marriage affords us great opportunities to forgive and to be forgiven. The close physical proximity in which we live has caused many of us to stumble over each other. Differences of ideas and the methods we use to express these ideas, coupled with the emotional vulnerability that is inherent in intimacy, cause many of us to act and react in ways that require forgiveness. In a spiritual sense, it is turning from God and living in fear that also provides ample opportunity for forgiveness.

I had an attorney friend once tell me that a couple living one hour together have generally offended each other enough times to warrant a divorce. Forgiveness requires us to believe in the redemptive powers of a loving God and, through our spiritual practice, to demonstrate these principles in our daily living. Forgiving is not the process of an eye for an eye. Forgiveness causes us to rise above the frail human condition that sanctions such behaviors and enables us to express our belief in God by turning the other cheek. Forgiveness is a choice; it accepts the gravity of the situation and seeks not justice, but compassion and mercy. It accepts the suffering involved, practices acceptance, patience, and tolerance, and exemplifies the courage to act without regard to one's own pain. It seeks neither retribution nor revenge. Forgiveness promotes healing and the restoration of peace. It avoids the pitfalls of anger, resentment, and bitterness of spirit. It seeks to bring the presence of God into the situation not with the intent of change, but with the humility of acceptance.

A great example of this process in current times occurred in the Amish community when in October 2006, a deranged man entered a school house in Lancaster, Pennsylvania, and tied up and shot eleven young girls, killing five of them. What greater provocation could a community have for anger towards God and towards the perpetrator? Instead, however, this Amish community turned towards God and sought to care for the surviving children, to bury their dead, and to forgive the perpetrator. In spite of their own grief, they were still able to offer solace and comfort to the killer's family, to restore peace and tranquility in their community, and to reestablish their efforts to educate their children. This capacity to forgive came from their conviction and belief in the God of their understanding. This provides a shining example for all of us who seek to forgive and be forgiven and seek the peace that flows from acts of forgiveness.

For many of us, the need for forgiveness is rooted in our own self-centeredness. It begins with a turning away from the practice of God's will in our lives. It seeks external gratification at the expense of our serenity and our relationship with God. The distractions that are presented to us by people, places, and things, or the feelings of fear, inadequacy or desire have caused many of us to live outside of our personal spiritual conviction and to violate our own boundaries. We have lived so many years in active addiction that it became natural for us to behave in this way.

In recovery we have come to believe that God can free us from the powerlessness of our addiction, restore us to sanity, and set us on the path to healthy living. These drastic changes in our lives are what precipitate our belief that God is loving. It is in the spirit of love that we learn kindness, patience, understanding, and long-suffering. It allows us to put the welfare of others above our self-centeredness.

To seek forgiveness or to forgive begins with a decision. It requires a turning away from self and a turning towards God. It reaffirms our belief that God can heal the situation at hand if we are willing to allow Him to do so. It is through the acceptance of our responsibility for our actions and their consequences that this happens. The self-centeredness that causes us to harm is the same self-centeredness that we must overcome in order to forgive. Turning to God allows us to turn away from the behaviors that have caused us and others great pain. This turning to God helps us to overcome unhealthy desires and replaces fear with love. A belief in God allows us to heal from the pain caused by guilt and self-obsession. It turns us away from undesired behaviors. It is turning to God that allows us to accept the pain of the situation, restores our ability to believe, reestablishes faith, dismisses resentments, encourages healing and overcomes the fear of being hurt again. It allows us to act in the spirit of love.

Our faith in God helps us make the changes necessary to forgive and be forgiven. It establishes a spirit of conversation that allows one to acknowledge one's wrongs and to practice behaviors that strengthen and renew the relationship. It also allows the person who is forgiving to practice behaviors that exemplify forgiveness. It allows us to be kind and to live in the present moment rather than in the pain of the past. Finally, it allows for reassessment and a renewed commitment to the practice of behaviors that strengthen one's pledge to the relationship and to a life of integrity.

Vigilance requires the person seeking forgiveness to hold themselves to a high level of accountability, not one imposed by the person doing the forgiveness, but by one's internal willingness to submit one's behaviors to God. It is in practicing these behaviors that we honor and strengthen the relationship. It requires the same diligence with which one practices the tenth step. Vigilance on the part of the person extending forgiveness requires them to search their own behavior for signs of anger, resentment, revenge, or retribution. It asks the forgiver, "Am I truly living in the spirit of my higher power, and am I practicing the principles of love"?

One of the obstacles to forgiveness is an unwillingness to change. Repeatedly seeking forgiveness without an expectation for change allows us to continue to dwell in the insanity of the situation. This desire to continue negative behaviors, while seeking to avoid consequences for those behaviors, ultimately leads to the destruction of the relationship. Such devastation of a relationship is often caused by conflict and guilt. The refusal to change is an unwillingness to accept that our behaviors have caused others to lose trust and to suffer unjustly. When we fail to change when change is called for, we are attempting to justify our will rather than accept the will of God. Through this, we are dishonoring our commitment to live in partnership with another.

Behaviors rooted in the disease of addiction seek to change our focus from accepting responsibility towards shifting guilt to another person. My wife refers to this practice as "Hocus pocus, change the focus." It is the insanity of repeating the same behaviors while hoping for a positive outcome. When our focus shifts from reality to mere perceptions, we deny the pain and anger caused by our actions, and we demonstrate a refusal to accept the responsibility. Our disease seeks in an unhealthy way to justify the behaviors of others which have caused us harm, rather than having us ask them for an acknowledgment of these wrongs. Accepting responsibility for the behaviors of others causes us unwarranted shame. Trying to assume control of another person's behaviors in an effort to maintain the relationship, rather than having the courage to assume the risk is a recipe for failure. This failure to act to preserve one's own sense of safety and to continue to live with unmanageability in our own lives causes us to change our focus from love to fear.

The act of asking for forgiveness requires humility and a turning towards God. It is an honest desire to accept the consequences of our own behavior and to acknowledge the pain that these behaviors caused. It is the desire to make amends and to reconcile the partners to a relationship with God. It is the intent to reestablish peace and harmony. It is the desire to live without self-obsession or fear. It is through acknowledgment of the offense and the harm that it has caused that one finds the nature of the wrong. Often at its core are fear and self-centeredness. Forgiveness involves choosing the appropriate time to ask for forgiveness. It allows for the feelings of the other person who has been affected to regain their own spiritual balance and to come to the spirit of forgiveness at their own pace. It allows time for a demonstration of one's personal change. Patience is a spiritual principle that must be practiced when seeking forgiveness.

Acknowledging the need for forgiveness may be done in private, quiet conversation, or in the presence of those who may have also suffered from the effects of our negative behavior, such as our families or the community at large. In some sense, a public apology is an affirmation of the desire to be in the relationship. The question of public or private amends is best answered by assessing the benefit to the relationship.

The act of forgiveness establishes and/or strengthens our ability to love. It also acknowledges that all is forgiven. It helps us establish and maintain our best behaviors. It helps us overcome an obsessive-compulsive fixation with the wrongs done and again focuses us on loving one another. At its best, forgiveness reestablishes God as the ultimate and loving authority in our lives.

In my spiritual seeking I have read accounts that acknowledge both our need for God and God's need for us. I have often thought in my own life that God needs me very much, because without someone like me, what would he do with all that forgiveness. God knows that throughout the years I have used up a lot of it!

Thoughts

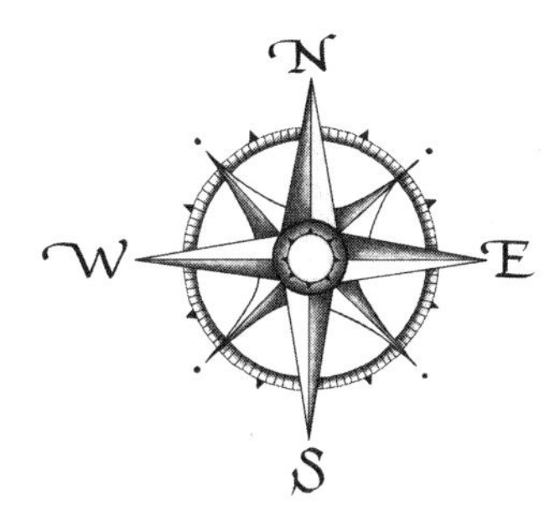

Chapter 15
Establishing Intimate Relationships

"Love is when the child in you invites the child in me out to play."
–R. McK

The following categories of character and social abilities and the respective questions may help assess your preparedness for entering into a relationship.

1. ***An established sense of self***

   - Have you established a sense of self?
   - Do you have a personal program of recovery?
   - Do you look to the other person to define who you are?
   - Does your happiness depend more on what others think of you or what you think of yourself?

2. ***Ability to maintain boundaries***

- Are you able to establish boundaries?
- Do you do things that are against your personal beliefs in order to maintain the relationship?
- Do you endure humiliation or shame at the hands of others?

3. *Personal integrity*

    - Are you able to live with personal integrity? Are you capable of trusting and are you trustworthy?

4. *Ties to old relationships*

    - Are you free emotionally from the effects of old relationships sufficiently enough to enter into new ones?
    - Do you try to reestablish past relationships with others in order to "fix yourself" in moments of uncertainty?
    - Do you fear losing the relationship enough to be manipulative and dishonest?

5. *Fear of Abandonment*

    - Do feelings of abandonment require you to be controlling of others?
    - Does this fear cause you to seek constant reassurance?

6. *Self-Control*

    - Are you able to control yourself enough to be able to express your feelings without hurting others?

7. *Irreconcilable differences*

    - Do you understand what your irreconcilable differences (deal breakers) may be such as religious beliefs, sexual or lifestyle incompatibilities, the desire for children or conflicts in the practice of personal beliefs?

8. *Motives, preparedness*

- Are your motives for entering a relationship healthy?
- Are you seeking to establish a mutually beneficial relationship?
- Have you established the belief that intimate and long-term relationships are possible?
- Do you seek advice from people who believe in relationships, or people who don't believe in relationships?

Understanding yourself in light of these issues will provide you with the basis for evaluating potential partners. This leads us to a discussion on the purpose of dating.

"Come away with me, for lo, the winter is past, the rains are over and gone, the flowers are showing in the fields, and the time for the singing of birds has come."
–Songs of Solomon

In the thinking that preceded the writing of this chapter I realized that I probably would have been able to share more experience if I entitled it, "How to capture and hold a lover hostage." In the self-centeredness of addiction, the fear of loss and the feeling of insecurity made it extremely difficult, if not impossible, to present myself factually or to accept others at face value. A history of failed relationships left me with an unconscious perception that *any* relationship would be of limited duration. It is only through working the steps and practicing the spiritual principles that I was able to develop a sense of self and the integrity necessary to develop intimacy.

Through the surrender of self-centeredness I became able to assess my motives when entering relationships. I learned to be a giver as well as a taker. In establishing personal boundaries, I became able to recognize potential irreconcilable differences before becoming romantically involved. I came to believe the core of all healthy relationships emanates from finding the beauty of love in a relationship first with a higher power, and then with others. It is out of this belief that I learned to risk my feelings without the fear of rejection.

I can remember praying out of the spirit of loneliness that God would send me someone with whom to share my life. When God presented me with the woman to whom I have been married for over 30 years, my first reaction was to live out of my disease and to establish all the reasons for why it would not work: age differences, blending families, differing political and social views, economics, etc. The acknowledgment of this relationship as a gift from a higher power did not come until I surrendered my unrealistic personal expectations, came to believe that our differences were in fact our strengths, and made a public commitment through the act of marriage to share our lives on a daily basis with the possibility that it would last forever.

A working knowledge of the steps allowed me to self-evaluate and to live with integrity. It allowed for the acceptance of my character defects and to live with the character defects of others without feelings of anger, resentment, or bitterness. It allowed me to seek forgiveness and to forgive, to be aware, and to seek through meditation and prayer to love and be loved.

The process of dating, for most, begins in adolescence. However, many of us in recovery, who are seeking to rebuild shattered lives, find that intimacy and the answer to love and belonging again becomes a process with which to achieve these ends. What makes it difficult for many of us is the fear of rejection. In an effort to stem the pain associated with this rejection, we developed unhealthy strategies for coping. In evaluating the strategies that we have used in the past that have proved unsuccessful, we might begin with clarifying in our own minds what it is that we hope to achieve through the dating process. Are we approaching dating solely as a social activity, as a means of answering our own sexual desires, or as the possibility to build and share a mutually beneficial life with another person?

We need to ask ourselves if we believe in the possibility of a long-term relationship for ourselves. While all of us in the dating process seek to put our best foot forward, are we being ourselves and factually presenting who we are, what we believe, and what our intentions are? We need to ask ourselves if we are being chameleon-like, by being what we think the other person wants us to be, rather than being who we really are.

In the past, many of us have rushed into physical intimacy, without regard to the consequences, as a way to cement or hold together the relationship. We bypass the anxiety often associated with getting to know others in a social setting that requires conversation. We tend to overlook the time necessary to develop friendship and unity. We often move towards physical intimacy before we are able to achieve intellectual, emotional, or spiritual safety. Instead of rushing towards an intimate, one on one relationship it may be helpful to participate in group activities where conversation and getting to know one another becomes a simple process, where a feeling of safety can be acquired. This allows us to enter conversations and to disclose feelings we don't normally consider to be part of developing an intimate relationship.

A historical perspective of relationships indicates prescribed rituals for courtship and marriage. Often decisions on who should marry were not made by individual couples but rather by parents, who thought decisions of such consequence should not be left to the young and inexperienced. It was often thought that emotions should be contained between couples until after they were betrothed. It exemplified the understanding that emotions would follow intellect. While in today's society the rituals of matchmaking and prearranged marriages have given way to free-choice, the decision to marry now rests with the couples.

While we have moved away from formal rituals it may be well noted that what we wish to preserve from those rituals was the concept of putting intelligence before emotions and the realization that love begets commitment, and the commitment to love produces intimacy and lasting relationship. Unity is not acquired through marriage; it should exist before being married, with marriage being the vehicle for public acknowledgment of a couple's devotion and the desire to live in accordance with the will of the God of their understanding.

In assessing our preparedness for intimacy, we might want to ask ourselves the following questions. We should ask these both of ourselves and of the person we hope to engage in a relationship.

- Am I prepared to present myself simply and factually to another person?

- Am I willing to be considerate of everyone's feelings in the relationship?

- If I were not physically attracted to this person, would I want to have a friendship with them?

- Would the friendship be one that could grow into a passionate affair?

- Does the person I am seeking to date work a program of recovery?

- Are they accepted in their own social circle?
- Do they respect others?
- Do they demonstrate the capacity for independence?
- Do they have the capacity to be nurturing?
- Does this person live their life with integrity?
- Is he/she of service to others?
- Does this individual practice manageability in his or her life?
- Does this person have any issues or beliefs significantly different from my own to constitute irreconcilable differences?
- Is this person capable of making and keeping commitments?
- Does he/she possess flexibility in thoughts and behaviors enough to reach a compromise if necessary?
- Does this individual present any defects of character that would cause me to feel unsafe or to cause insecurity in the relationship?
- Is there sexual compatibility?
- Can I accept this person's preexisting responsibilities to children, parents, financial resources, etc.?

Thoughts

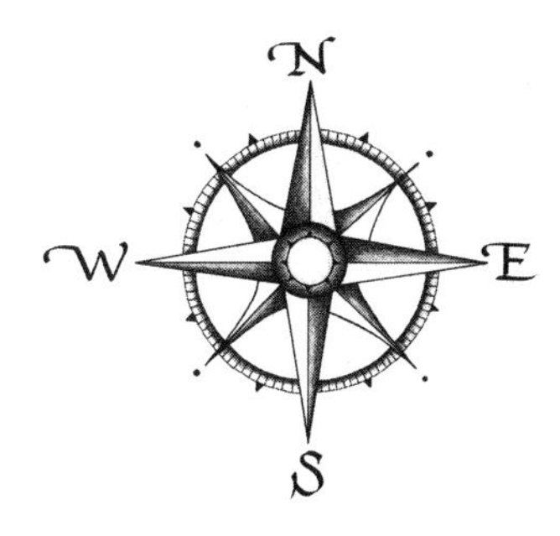

Chapter 16
Making the Commitment

"In marriage you are not sacrificing yourself to the other person.
You are sacrificing yourself to the relationship."
–Joseph Campbell

In our third step we learn to make decisions, to honor commitments, and to turn to a higher power as a source of strength. In our third tradition we establish our rights to membership. The only right or requirement for entering into a relationship is the desire to do so. We know that desire provides a tremendous amount of strength and willingness.

While some people possess great musical ability, with perfect pitch and terrific music memory, they might not play any instruments because they lack the desire to do so. Then there are many people who play music exceptionally well because they have the desire to learn and the commitment to practice. My friend who is a music teacher keeps a set of rosary beads in his teaching area. When one of his students is not committed to practicing, he hands them the rosary beads with the instructions to pray for divine intervention; without practice, divine intervention provides the only hope.

When considering entry to a relationship, one needs to ask one's self whether the decision to do so is a conscious or unconscious decision. Many of us enter relationships based solely on physical attraction and passion. Others of us continue to pick the same type of partners habitually, often getting the same results: failure. A conscious decision requires us to follow a process which reviews past history; it requires us to ask ourselves why our past relationships have failed.

- Is it because we choose people with whom it is impossible to have a lasting relationship because they are unable to honor their own commitments (i.e. being married while still engaging in other relationships)?

- Is the other person fully available emotionally?

- Do they possess the resources and strengths in their own life to make a relationship possible?

- Do we have unrealistic expectations of what a relationship should or should not provide?

- Have we ourselves achieved a sense of independence and completed the developmental tasks previously outlined in Chapter 12?

- Do we truly believe it is possible for us to have a loving relationship, or do we hold the deep seeded belief that we are unworthy of one?

- If we still harbor feelings of unworthiness or the inability to be loved, has our behavior contributed to a self fulfilling prophecy? *Sometimes these feelings are masked by ego-driven behaviors.*

- Do we rely solely on our ability to attract people physically; are we able to show others who we really are intellectually, emotionally, and spiritually?

- Do we still practice the shaming behaviors (i.e. putting people down, belittling past relationships, speaking ill of their families, etc.)?

The decision making process consciously gathers facts, assesses the past, and invites others involved into the process. It assesses the requirements for fulfilling the decision and considers the consequences of the decision. Non-conscious decision making can be habitual, impulsive, and done with little or no thought.

An example of both types can be illustrated simply by looking at how we tie our shoes. Most of us don't even have to think about how we do this task—we just bend down and tie them. But if we teach this task to others or wish to evaluate effectiveness, we need to bring it to a conscious level where we can ask ourselves how it is we do what we do. Consciousness practiced in decision making allows us to accept responsibility for the consequences of our actions and provides a learning experience by assessing the outcome. In our third step we turn our will and our lives over to the care of God. Practicing this in a relationship allows us to behave lovingly.

Turning our will over to the care of God as we understand Him provides us with a set of beliefs which can guide our behavior in a relationship. Turning over our will is turning to God as a source of strength to help us understand how to love and to be loved. It is commitment and a path to success. It is the belief that no matter what happens we can get through it together. It is a belief that the resources that are necessary for our success will be provided to us by a loving God. It is the understanding that if we do our part, God will do his. Turning our will over to the care of God allows us to take ownership for the relationship with the belief that it will be a lasting one.

Trusting God in the relationship requires that we practice specific behaviors like those previously outlined in the discussion of Corinthians 1:13 in Chapter One. In praying for knowledge of God's will, we find direction, strength, and an ability to practice those beliefs. Praying is not a passive action limited solely to an intellectual process. Praying for knowledge requires a review of the past and seeks out the experience of those who have what we want: in this instance, loving long-term relationships. Praying may also include reviewing literature on loving and relationship, seeking professional help, and most importantly, prayer encourages the practice of spiritual principals.

Some of us find it helpful to write about our past relationships and make a list of their positive and negative characteristics. This provides a format for discussing them with others. It is often said that *a man with an opinion is no match for a man with an experience.* We ask ourselves who are the people in our lives that have good long-term relationships? What questions would we want to ask them? Although we provide you with some written examples in Chapter 21, we encourage you to think this out and make your own list of questions. Most people who have a loving relationship find it easy to love others and are willing to share what works for them.

Another requirement is a willingness on your part to approach others with your questions. In reviewing the literature it may be helpful to begin the search within the constructs of your own spiritual beliefs. If the answers aren't there, you can feel free to broaden the search. Loving is the strong common thread that runs through most religious or spiritual paths.

Our higher power is the engine of love. He provides the strength required to endure and overcome adversity. This power is demonstrated in a willingness to learn and to practice the behaviors that are conducive to developing intimacy and trust. Our higher power gives us the ability to overcome our self-interest and substitute self-sacrifice for the benefit of others. It provides us the ability to be tender, kind, giving, and patient without requiring it of others. The God of our own understanding allows us to risk and to be vulnerable to the possibilities that intimacy requires. The little acts of loving that we practice every day reveal our belief in a higher power.

Some of us are pushed by our inadequacies to want the grandiose but short-lived behaviors. I said to my wife one day that I would really like to do something to change the world. She suggested that I start by taking out the trash. It is these little acts of making coffee, helping with the cleaning and sharing the responsibilities of maintaining a home that truly demonstrate one's commitment. Practicing these behaviors support great relationships.

For addicts, it is extremely difficult to feel loved, the vulnerability is sometimes overwhelming. Our third tradition says the only requirement is desire. If we have presented ourselves honestly and believe that the other party has done the same, then we do not have to fear exposure. In unhealthy relationships, people have entered them for reasons of self-centeredness or fear. Self-centeredness is often as innocent as the desire to be served, as innocuous as asking people to do everything for you, or as blatant as a desire to perform sexually when there is no mutual desire or satisfaction to be achieved. Self-centeredness may be born out of the fear of being alone. It is seen when our behavior is meant only for self gratification.

There is a common theme with those who have suffered parental abandonment. It is born out of the fear that one cannot take care of oneself. It is entering into relationships solely for emotional and financial benefits. Healthy desire is expressed in relationships by a willingness to love as well as to be loved and to love others without self-interest. It is to share responsibility for the health of the relationship. It is to risk vulnerability to develop intimacy. It is a willingness to put the time and energy into the relationship and allows time for fun and romance. It is being there for each other when life on life's terms is painful, difficult or joyful.

There are those of us who have been traumatized by our past feelings of vulnerability. These feelings often keep us from wanting to commit fully. And yet, as the line in Bette Midler's *The Rose* says, "It's the soul afraid of dying that never learns to live." Trust is at the very core of any relationship. When I was a child my old Irish grandmother used to say that she never had to punish me for lying because the punishment was the inability to believe or to trust others or the integrity to trust oneself. Hopefully we have progressed far enough in our recovery to believe that recovery is possible in spite of our past failures and attempts to stay clean. It is in the knowledge of this possibility that we learn to trust God and accept being loved.

In the same fashion that we trust God in our personal recovery, we trust God in the emotional risk that loving requires. In the past some of us have been in relationships where trust has been betrayed and we have been hurt. We have paid the price for choosing poorly. Yet it is only the ability to again give of oneself openly and fully that allows intimacy to be achieved. While failure to achieve intimacy in a relationship can be painful, if we practice spiritual principles, we are able to count on two things. First that it is possible for us to have a loving relationship, and second it may be an indication that God may have something or someone better in mind for us.

Love and relationship require us to assume many different roles. For example, consider that we can assume the role of a caretaker in times of illness, the role of a friend in times of disappointment, a parent in times of need for nurturing, and a child when needing nurturing ourselves. Awareness of these roles allows us to achieve balance in our relationship. It can be destructive and unhealthy when we relate to each other from only one role.

Thoughts

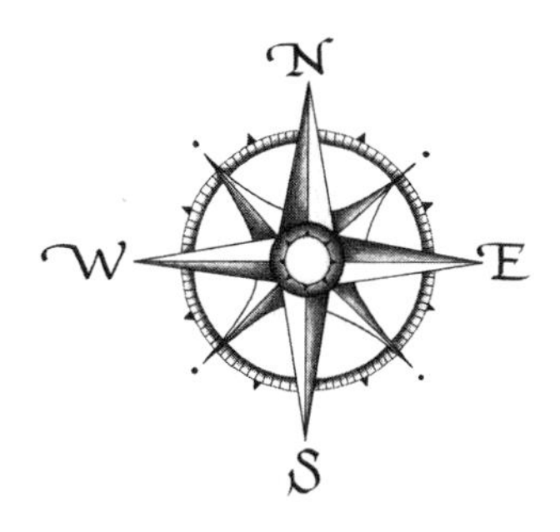

Chapter 17

Defining Relationships Through Inventory

"Most can see other people's faults. A few can see other people's virtues. Only one or two can see their own shortcomings."
–Ancient Sanskrit Verse

The title of this work identifies the type of relationship that most of us seek—an intimate one. Yet, what is it we seek in intimacy? Is it the warmth of physical touch, fulfillment of sexual desire, or the simplicity of the held hand? Perhaps it is the freedom to share our most perplexing questions with one another or our innermost thoughts. Could it be the intense emotional feelings and desire of belonging? Or is it seeking spiritual expression through the unity of spirits or a binding of souls to God and to each other? Could it be our calling to love?

The *Winston Dictionary* defines intimacy as "confidential fellowship." In recovery our public expression of an intimate relationship is often shown through our participation in a 12 step program. It requires only the desire for membership. Membership rests solely with the individual. The manifestations of this desire are often seen in honesty, open-mindedness, willingness, and an acknowledgment of our personal responsibility for our behavior. While membership shuns outward authority, it accepts an internal sense of authority. The second tradition defines this authority for us as a loving God. While a personal understanding and image of God may be of one's own choosing, the commonality of understanding that leads to intimacy requires that God be loving. Turning one's will over to the care of God is an act of submission.

An intimate relationship requires no less a commitment and no less than acceptance of the personal responsibility for the well-being of that relationship. It should be held with the same sanctity and sacredness that one offers to a loving God. Ancient scripture speaks of two spiritual concepts, submission and sacrifice, both of which require a willingness to lay down one's life for the other. This can be as grandiose as the willingness to take a bullet, or as simple as completing the daily chores of making coffee and taking out the trash.

It is in the nature of our disease that some of us have found ourselves lost in self-centeredness. We need not remain there if we have a willingness to take our fourth step. In this process some of us have found ourselves locked in the unhealthy thinking of intimacy as the passion for sexual conquest, intellectual mind-games, and trying to attain the unattainable by engaging in relationships with others who profess to be in an existing relationship.

Because of unhealthy emotional needs or fear of loneliness, some of us have clung to abusive relationships—physical, emotional, or shaming. Some of us remain locked in spiritual hoping, seeking the fulfillment of our own desires rather than the willingness to accept God's desire for us. Some of us stand at the station waiting for a train that will never come, refusing to accept what God so willingly puts before us.

A story that illustrates this is one of a man trapped in the rising waters of a flood. As they rise, a neighbor comes by on a four wheeler and offers to carry him to safety. He says, "No, I'm putting my trust in God"! As the waters rise higher another neighbor floats by in a boat and also offers help. The man again replies, "No, I'm trusting in God"! As the water gets higher and he is on top of his roof, a helicopter appears overhead and a voice says, "Grab the rope and let me pull you to safety"! The man again responds that he is waiting and trusting in God. He then proceeds to drown.

Awakening, he finds himself in the presence of God, at which point he asks Him, "How could you let this happen to me? I trusted you fully and completely"! Whereupon God replies, "I sent you a four wheeler, I sent you a boat, I sent you a helicopter. I can only help those who are truly willing to accept my help."

At the core of intimacy is longing. Longing presupposes a fulfillment, an ability to be one with God's will, a coming home of the spirit, and finding peace in our soul. Sharing this longing with another human being offers the possibility that the two shall become as one, where death holds no fear, and where every sacrifice required of the relationship can be met. Oral traditions and literature have recorded many instances where couples have chosen to die together rather than to live apart. Yet, we hear in stories about divorce of people who have simply drifted apart. One wonders if this is because partners remain each in their own boat rather than being in one boat. It is much more difficult to drift apart if people are in the same boat. How do we step out of our boat of individuality into a common boat called relationship? How do we establish boundaries and identity for our relationship?

Perhaps it is because of the practice of spiritual principles and a spiritual awakening that we found in the 12 steps. Practicing these principles provides us with the integrity to be who we say we are and do what we say we will do. Strength of character allows us to surrender personal desires for common welfare, and precipitate a willingness to sacrifice for the common good. The paradox found in these spiritual principles allows for each relationship to be uniquely individual while developing a sameness of spirit.

While this book does not seek to find a relationship for you, its hope is to illuminate and provide you with some spiritual principles through which you can establish relationship boundaries and a compass that will allow you to find the port of love in the midst of a storm.

Relationships are a partnering of individuals for mutual benefit. With couples it requires a sharing of responsibility in providing the basic necessities for survival (i.e., food, clothing, shelter, transportation, etc.). Partnering is the division of labor required for maintaining the home. It is a sharing of ideas which provides intellectual stimulation. It is providing emotional support for each other during difficult times. Partnering enhances the understanding of God in each other and in the relationship.

In establishing boundaries in your relationship, here are some questions you may wish to ask yourself:

- Is our home a place of peace and of safety?

- In our discussions, are we being open-minded or trying to make a point?

- What are the barriers to intimacy? Are we trying to reach a common understanding with our significant other?

- How do we demonstrate honesty, open-mindedness,

and willingness to find common ground?

- Do we demonstrate the behaviors we like to see in others?
- Are we being self-righteous and more intent on winning arguments than we are on sustaining the relationship?
- Are we practicing our personal spiritual principles?
- What is the cost of our behavior to the relationship?
- Do our individual behaviors demonstrate a unity of purpose?
- What diverts us from being loving?
- Do we trust God to help us find the strength to do the right things? How do we do this?
- What is our part and what is God's part in finding a solution? Are we doing our part?
- What is the likely outcome of our present behaviors?
- Have we reached an impasse where we need to seek direction outside of ourselves?
- Are we willing to work to a mutually acceptable outcome? How do we demonstrate our patience in this process?
- Are we living in the present or are we resorting to old negative behaviors?
- What spiritual beliefs help us find our common welfare?
- Do we let others negatively affect our relationship? (i.e., parents, children, or our recovering community)
- Do we practice self-enhancement at the expense of our spouse by being shaming or blaming?

- Do we disclose private and confidential issues to others?
- Do we try to build consensus with others who practice rat packing behaviors (in an effort to exert pressure on our spouse to surrender to our will)?
- Do we support each other in individual achievements while growing together as a couple?
- Have we learned to disagree without being disagreeable?
- How do we demonstrate that we respect, comfort, and love each other?
- Is there a consistency of commitment in our relationship?
- Are there commonly held values that allow for individual expression yet offer continued support and intimacy and strengthen the relationship?
- Do we share responsibilities and divide the labor necessary to make the relationship work?
- Do we share ideas?
- Do we involve each other in the planning and making of decisions?
- Do we share the details of our lives with each other, even mundane issues of work or school?
- Do we listen to what the other has to share with us?
- Do we intellectually stimulate each other by sharing readings, poems, or concepts that hold our interest?
- Do we enjoy recreation and have fun together?
- Do we set aside quiet, decision-making time for just the two of us?

- Do we still go on dates?
- Do we allow each other moments of being less than?
- Do we share our spiritual seeking?
- Do we honor each other by remembering holidays, anniversaries, and other special events?
- Do we dream together and share common visions of the future?
- Do we practice behaviors that allow each individual to feel secure?
- Does the child in me invite the child in you out to play?

Thoughts

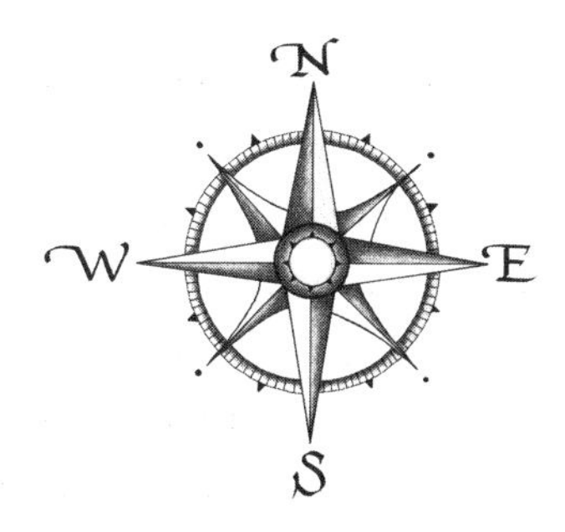

Chapter 18
One Life Lived Well

"It is the mark of a great man that he puts to flight all ordinary calculations. He is at once sublime and touching, childlike, and of the race of giants."
–Honoré de Balzac

Establishing an environment of safety in the relationship allows us to nurture one another. It allows the relationship to fulfill its purpose. A quote from the basic text of Narcotics Anonymous found in tradition five states, "Unity of action makes possible what seems impossible for us—recovery." The demands of living a shared life while working a program of recovery, continuing our personal education, fulfilling our vocational requirements, raising children, providing service to the community at large, participating in the social and cultural activities of our children, and possibly supporting parents, can seem daunting, if not impossible, tasks. These stressors can bring on feelings of inadequacy. It's as if we're running as fast as we can but staying in the same place, perhaps even moving backwards. Sometimes it is possible for us to become overwhelmed with accepting life on life's terms with all of the tasks required of us.

A nurturing environment begins with recognizing the amount of time and labor necessary to support a family. It requires each person in the relationship to recognize the efforts of the other and to lift up, motivate, support, and nurture. The stress that often accompanies everyday tasks can sometimes cause us to target others as a way of providing personal relief. Sometimes in our pursuit of perfection we judge ourselves and others too harshly. We lose sight of the power of a loving God in the relationship. This has caused many of us to become vulnerable to outside negative influences. Some of the behaviors associated with this are seeking comfort in past negative behaviors or trying to reestablish old, unhealthy relationships. This lack of integrity on our part often begins in small ways. It is a lie to think that we can take comfort in these negative behaviors from our past without paying a terrible price and suffering the consequences.

Many relationships are destroyed because we cannot find the security that truth offers. Lying often begins in small ways, such as convincing ourselves that we can achieve something for nothing. Many of us have lost sight of the fact that truth is what sets us free. When the spirit of truth leaves us, the spirit of harmony and love quickly follows. When we separate ourselves from a higher power, we become vulnerable to the lies of others. Without the inner strength of God we make ourselves vulnerable to flattery and ego-enhancing statements from others who seek to exploit us. In the loss of self-honesty we become exceptionally vulnerable to deception, both from ourselves and from others. This often results in self-exploitation and a willingness to become the victim.

While there is usually only one truth, there are many forms of deception. When we move away from our capacity to love, it is replaced by a fear of losing, of not getting enough, and of our deception being exposed. This plunges us into the triangle of self-obsession. When we put our own desires before the welfare of the relationship, we put the relationship at great risk.

Many of us have begun by lying about money. Our inability to manage resources properly has caused great stress in maintaining relationships and is one of the greatest sources of conflict. Our addiction makes us vulnerable to trying to fix our emotional stress or unhappiness through unwarranted spending. Faith in a higher power, however, allows us to practice the spiritual paradox that sometimes to have less is to have more.

When people in a relationship get involved sexually or emotionally with others outside of the relationship, focus of their desire changes from the welfare of their home to values practiced in the street. Sexual impropriety always begins with a lie. This often leaves people feeling betrayed and shatters the trust that is at the core of intimacy. The surrender of truth is the root of destruction in relationships.

We now ask ourselves how we can develop a level of intimacy in a relationship. I propose that it begins with integrity, which is essentially the awareness of the power and consequences of the words that flow from our mouths. It is establishing core values that emanate from our understanding of a loving God and pursuing a sense of humility. Integrity focuses on living from internal God-centered values. It is the recognition that peace of mind is far more valuable than external pleasures. It is comforting each other with the knowledge that God does exist in the relationship. A relationship maintains its security by providing truth, integrity and confidentiality. The disclosure of confidences can cause intense feelings of shame. Avoiding the pitfalls of being the victim, of being put upon are made evident through living with integrity and trustworthiness.

While it is often said that discretion is the better part of valor, truth is also often the path to freedom. Integrity is the cornerstone of security. While we have a right to privacy, secrets have the power to take us back into the misery of addiction. How much to disclose to one another in a relationship should be assessed by the ability of the information to harm the other person. One should consider whether disclosure will strengthen or weaken the relationship. This is akin to the requirements of making amends in step nine: "We made amends to such people, wherever possible, *except when to do so would injure them or others.*" (Ninth Step).

When we are unclear about what or how much we should disclose, some of us have found it helpful to discuss this with a confidante, be it a sponsor with whom we have established trust, or with a professional for whom confidentiality is a required ethical code of conduct. The energy required to live in deception often results in depression and has led more than one person to relapse or commit suicide. We seek to live our life fully with integrity and in companionship with someone with whom we have developed trust, intimacy, and the capacity to love.

At the beginning of a relationship, one should be free and willing to discuss areas that they believe would make the relationship impossible. Some people allowed strong emotional attachments to develop under the misconception that, "I waited until I could trust you to tell you these things," or in the erroneous belief that one can change the other person's way of thinking to one's own.

There are personally held values one may not be willing to surrender for the benefit of relationship. Issues of health that may put the other at risk (i.e., HIV, hepatitis C, STDs, infertility, etc.) need to be discussed immediately. Issues such as an unwillingness of one's partner to have children, an unwillingness to accept pre-existing responsibilities, such as physical handicaps, children from a previous relationship, etc., have caused many relationships to end. These hindrances may result from a rigidity rooted in culture, race, religion, or in an incapability of character. Perhaps it may be the inability to accept the emotional makeup of one's partner such as mood swings, anger, sexual incompatibility, or the requirement of some individuals to use medication. It may be an unwillingness to accept the spiritual expression of others because of one's own religious beliefs. This is an attitude that may be worth surrendering.

It is a dishonest approach and a self-deception to believe that one is ready for a new relationship while still clinging to a past one. This is a deception born out of vulnerability. In its most blatant form it is exploiting someone who you know is not capable of having a healthy relationship because of their situation in life—like when people in recovery prey on the newcomer.

In existing relationships, conflicts can occur when one or both partners squander the resources of the relationship as a fix for answering their emotional needs or self-interest, thereby sinking the relationship into the quandary of debt. The ensuing stress has caused many relationships to end or addicts to relapse. The withholding of emotional or sexual response to gain power and control in a relationship has often caused people to seek sexual or emotional gratification elsewhere.

An inability to honestly address these issues keeps a relationship in constant turmoil and leads to a collapse of intimacy. Honest communication and a God-centered approach to these issues can lead to a constructive resolution. Much can be revealed through looking into the eyes of another. It is not by power that we resolve issues; rather, it is in the spirit of quiet conversation and the humility to seek mutually acceptable outcomes. People need to communicate *with* each other rather than communicate *about* each other.

Thoughts

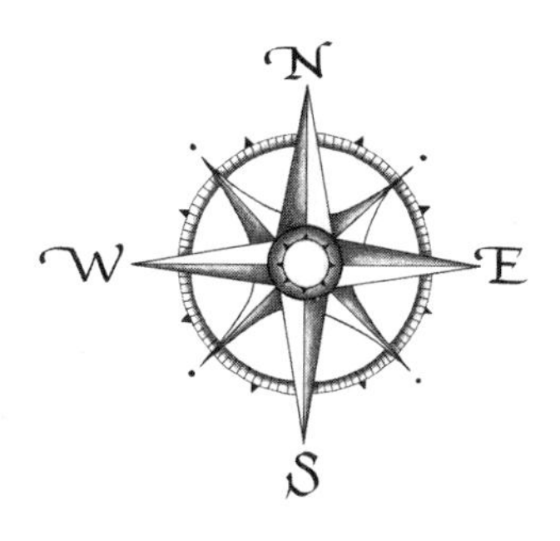

Chapter 19

Self-Acceptance & Dating (In That Order!)

When seeking your partner, if your intuition is a virtuous one, you will find him or her. If not, you will keep finding the wrong person.
–Joseph Campbell

In preparing for a personal relationship some of us have found it beneficial to develop the following things:

- a working knowledge of the twelve steps and twelve traditions;
- a sponsor with whom we have a personal relationship;
- a support network (including a home group and friends with whom we socialize); and
- a spiritual identity.

We also may have reestablished relationships with our families, and some of us have sought professional help. In developing a support network for our relationships we look to role models, couples who show mutual respect and love for each other. We seek to develop a peer group or social circle of couples who endeavor to have long-term relationships. We seek to establish individually or together those spiritual connections that support the concept of relationships. We make use of parents or surrogate parents, people who have long-term relationships and a willingness to share honestly and openly the methods for their success. We may seek marriage counseling as well as counseling on issues of manageability such as money, sex, children, etc.

The process of dating is often new. While we may have had numerous partners in the past, the thought of being ourselves and sharing that with another can be challenging. So many times in the past we have been a chameleon, adapting to the values and behaviors of who we are with, without regard to who we are. The ability to present ourselves as we truly are often causes us anxiety. In the past we may have taken hostages, compromised our integrity, and diminished our self-worth as an escape from being alone. We have become masters of the short game, moving from partner to partner without ever being able to find fulfillment.

In self-acceptance we find the ability to be okay with ourselves and to accept others for who they are. Self-acceptance allows us a consistency of behavior that promotes trust. It is this trust that allows us to make the choices that foster intimate and long-term relationships. The boundaries of self-acceptance establish the behaviors we find acceptable or unacceptable. We no longer will allow ourselves to be mistreated.

We then eventually become prepared to enter a relationship as a partner bringing hopes, dreams, talents, and a capacity to love as well as to be loved. We find that we are no longer willing to settle for second best. We should have established what relationship incompatibilities (deal breakers) are, such as the desire for children, a code of values or beliefs, economic status, social, religious, spiritual, addiction, violence or cultural differences on which we are unwilling to compromise.

Thoughts

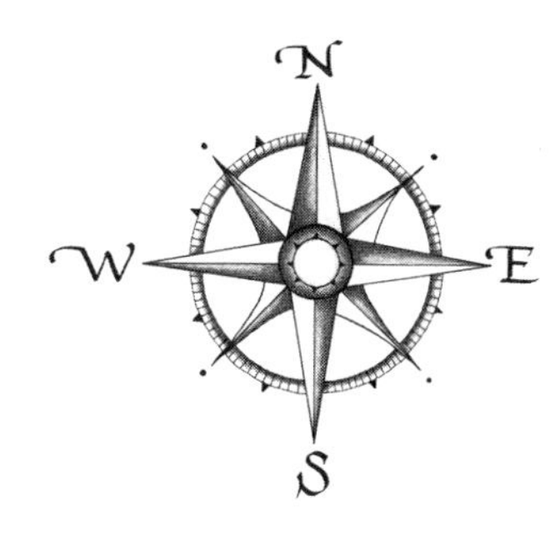

Chapter 20
Ending Relationships

"The price of love is that one will bury the other."
–Anonymous

In the recovery process nothing offers us the potential for relapse more than our inability to deal with the pain of loss. It is out of this understanding that we offer newcomers in recovery the suggestion that they avoid intimate relationships for at least their first year. Many of us, overwhelmed by feelings of longing, desire, or passion overlook the potential for pain that is inherent when we love others. What allows us to love in the face of death are the same spiritual principles that allow us to commit ourselves to relationships with the potential to end. In the practical sense we learn, through the practice of spiritual principles, to establish a sense of self and a belief in a higher power that provides us with the internal strength on which we can draw during times of loss and intense emotional pain. We learn to reach outside of ourselves and to draw strength from our relationships with our family, friends, sponsor, our home group, and our recovery fellowship. We learn to express our feelings of loss and to receive the nurturing from others that helps us to heal.

The process of grief, while most commonly thought of as a response to the loss felt in death, can universally be applied to any situation where one feels an overwhelming sense of loss. Elizabeth Kubler-Ross in her book "On Death and Dying," establishes a benchmark for understanding this process. For our purposes we will discuss the universal process of healing from feelings of loss from either the death of a significant other or from the loss felt when relationships end. The five stages of grief we will explore are denial, anger, negotiation, sadness, and moving on. Understanding these stages can help us to understand where we fall in the healing process.

When a loved one dies the healing process begins after the life has ended. However, in relationships that are ending, the process may begin to occur while the couple is still together. It has been my personal experience that women tend to grieve while still in the relationship while men do not begin to grieve until after the relationship has ended.

How this process tends to play out is that one partner recognizes a problem in the relationship. They may say, "We need to get help, things are not right," etc. The other person, who is in the stage of denial says, "You're overreacting, everything is okay, go about your business."

The person experiencing grief may move on to the next step which is anger. The person still in denial writes this off as the unreasonableness of the other person. They often refer to the other's anger as nagging or "bitching." In an effort to save the relationship, the person in the grief process may change themselves with the false hope that it may fix the relationship. When this proves insufficient due to the partner still in denial, this person may become depressed, uncommunicative, withdrawn, etc. This is akin to the period of mourning and loss.

The next stage for them is to say, "This is over, I'm out of here." This often leads to physical separation. The person still in denial may have difficulty realizing why the separation is happening. When their denial cracks, they begin to realize that outside help, counseling, etc. that may have actually been a good idea before, is no longer an option. When coming to this realization, they begin to feel angry at the loss and fail to understand that the other person has already worked through this. It is in this stage where there is a potential for threats, stalking, violence, abuse, or other unhealthy expressions of anger.

When moving on to the next stage this person apologizes, promises to change, and becomes willing to work things out. When this proves unfruitful, they then begin to feel depressed, withdrawn, and fearful. Many of us have chosen to express our depression in physically unhealthy ways such as overeating, gambling, or unhealthy sexual practices.

In unhealthy responses to grief, a person sometimes becomes stuck in one of the stages of grief and continues to practice unhealthy behaviors that derive from their pain. Hopefully in the process of moving on, they relinquish their feelings of bitterness and resentment, both of which are toxic to recovery. It is in the practice of forgiveness that we free ourselves from these feelings, establish emotional balance, and regain our joy of life.

The practice of the principles found in the steps, while in the grieving process, allows us to acknowledge the pain associated with loss, and helps us to develop the beliefs that make it possible for one to heal. This renews the capacity to love again. We become able to accept loss with dignity and live according to our spiritual beliefs. Self-examination allows us to examine our role in the relationship, to learn from our mistakes and to make amends when necessary. In instances of death, our spirituality helps us to remember how fully we are capable of loving.

In the ending of a relationship we examine our motives for entering the relationship and the criteria we used for choosing our partner. We examine the appropriateness of our conduct during the relationship and after it has ended. We learn to share our pain with others, and to relinquish feelings of anger and begin to forgive. We allow ourselves time to heal, and to learn to establish new criteria. We assess our readiness to enter a new relationship, and we learn to love again. It is in our trust in a higher power's will for us that we learn that we have nothing to fear. Nothing.

Thoughts

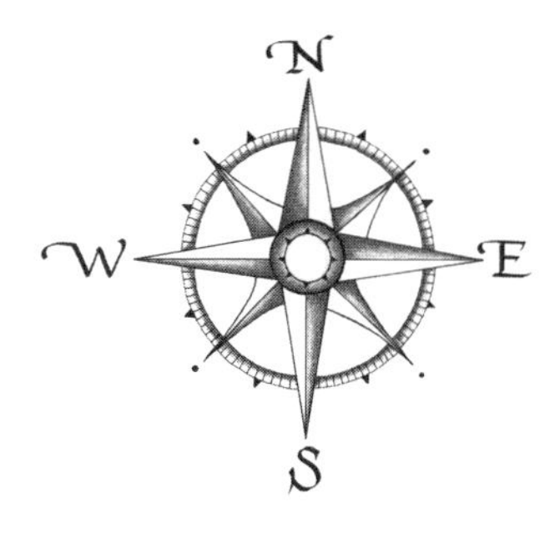

Chapter 21

Personal Stories about Intimacy & Relationships

"The beginning of love is to let those we love be
perfectly themselves, and not to twist them to fit our own image.
Otherwise, we love only the reflection of ourselves we find in them.
–Thomas Merton

The following chapter includes some of the responses I received from a questionnaire. I asked a limited number of people in recovery to answer. I thank those who responded. While their names have been changed to honor privacy, responses are printed with only minimal editing for ease in reading. In addition, there were those who felt their relationship was in such a state that they felt they had nothing to offer. There were also those whose sponsors suggested that they may not have sufficiently worked through their own issues enough to comment. I thank them also and hope that perhaps this work will be of some value to them.

Catherine and Paul

1. A brief Bio (age, sex, clean time etc.)

I am a 41 white female. I have 5-1/2 years clean. Mother of 5 and an only child.

2. Describe family origin.

I am an only child; came from a broken home (mother and father separated when I was 2 yrs old). I was tossed from family member to family member so I was moving around a lot. No living relatives left but my children.

3. List issues you would describe as dysfunctional.

Abandonment, addiction, co-dependency, anger, resentment, blame, unmanageability, no consistency or stability because of moving around all the time, my mom went from relationship to relationship.

4. How did/do you feel about your upbringing?

I used to feel abandoned and unwanted, and sad and angry. But today I feel that my family did the best they could with what they had. They just did what they were taught; today I am able to break the cycle. By letting go of the resentments that kept me angry, I am better able to move on. This helps me to arrive at the acceptance of them and me and to healing.

5. Were/are there any issues that have made relationships difficult for you?

Of course the abandonment, co-dependency, no self-worth, abuse.

6. How did you resolve them, or, how do you live with them if still unresolved?

The steps are what have helped me, and finding a GOD of my own understanding has nourished me through some issues. Most of all is through self love and looking within myself and being able to forgive. Forgiveness is the key to all issues for me. I took a look at my own life and my choices and how I wanted forgiveness for doing some of the same things that were done to me as a child and adult. I realize I cannot ask for something that I am not willing to give. I saw the cycle and realized it was not personal—it was the only thing we knew until I became teachable.

7. How would you describe an intimate, loving, nurturing relationship (utopian and real)?

Letting someone be who they truly are. Complete honesty and trust. Being friends and lovers is the most intimate experience I think a couple can share. Uncontainable love—freedom brings a couple closer.

8. How many times have you been married or in significant (long term) relationship?

I have been married twice in active addiction. I was always in a relationship. They weren't healthy, but I feel it was significant because they showed me what I did not want out of a relationship. Since I have been clean, I have only been in two relationships. In my early recovery, there was a very sick relationship, and for almost 4 years I've been with the man who is now my husband.

9. What did you learn about yourself and about relationships from these experiences?

I learned a lot about the fact that by being co-dependent, I was looking back on how I used to think that the more a person abused me and controlled me, the more they loved me. I was fearful of being left and I always depended on them to make me feel special and to fix me. I never took responsibility for my life. I had no beliefs of my own. In my marriage I have learned that self-love is the key to being in a healthy relationship. The more I am true to me the truer I can be to him.

10. How long are you currently married?

August 2008 will be one year, but we have lived together for almost four years.

11. What do you believe are the most important things in maintaining an intimate, loving, nurturing relationship?

What I learned is you must have a God of your own understanding, and that you must have self-love in order to love another. You must have honesty, trust, respect, freedom to be who you are, acceptance, and the ability to stay individuals.

12. What struggles have you overcome?

Wanting to fix my husband, not taking on his stuff, and allowing him the space to fix himself. Trust for me in the beginning was hard, but today I trust him completely because I trust myself today. I have overcome being co-dependent. Sometimes I still look to him to validate me.

13. How do you live with each other's defects of character?

I think this is where we really practice the program and acceptance. We know there is still work to be done, and that work is to be done with our sponsors—not with each other.

We know neither of us is perfect. Sometimes we can laugh at ourselves. We really do not act out on each other—that offends.

14. How do you handle conflict?

Believe it or not, we do not have a lot of conflict. But when it does come about, I take a moment to look within myself and to talk with GOD; then we talk. I think we really practice our belief that there is no right or wrong. I have the right to feel and see things the way I want to, and he has the same right. But we try to stay open to each other's way of looking at things and each other's feelings. And we are both quick to say "I am sorry" and stop the behavior if we do end up harming the other.

15. What are the strengths of your relationship?

GOD, THE 12 STEPS and TRADITIONS, Spiritual principles, Communication, TRUST, unconditional love.

16. How do you create private time in your relationship?

I think because we do stay individuals it has been easy for us to have private time. We each work our own program, and because we do not feel we have to ask the other one if we can do something, we make plans with friends and family. All the time and each of us have a choice if we want to go or stay home or do something else. So private time is really not an issue. I mean, don't get me wrong, we make plans with one another, but really we are always going places and doing things together and separately. I think we have a nice balance because we do practice freedom.

17. What are your happiest times together?

I love when we are lying in bed together at the end of a long day and I lay my head on his chest, and he rubs my head and I can hear his heart beat. (Not sure he would say the same). I also enjoy when one of us discover something new in our spiritual journey, to see our eyes light up. Those are the best moments for me, and when we spend family time.

18. How do you maintain romance and desire?

I think this is the lesson we are at in our relationship. I always desire my husband but my sex drive is not all that. So we have been discussing this area of our relationship. I think energy is the issue for me. I have gained a lot of weight so because I do not like the way I feel or look, I do not feel as sexy. And my energy level is low.

19. What spiritual beliefs does each individual in the relationship hold?

That we are all one and GOD is not out there somewhere, but within each of us. Everything we need is right inside of us, and we are all reflections of GOD.

20. What are your common spiritual beliefs?

We are all reflections of God and equal. Paul and I have the same belief. I think that is why we have such a peaceful relationship. Our belief is LOVE. We really try our best to come from a place of love and compassion. And we believe in the 12 steps.

21. What would you describe as fruits of your relationship?

Love, self-respect, trust, freedom, peace, honesty, family.

22. How does your relationship share with others?

My children see the love between us and they open their minds to practice the same things in their relationships that we practice. The first search for them was finding a loving God because they see God working in our life. My son told me one day (he had to stay with us for about 6 months), and he said it was first time in his life that he lived somewhere and no one raised their voice, he said, "You two never argue, why is that"? He saw us pray together and mediate. He saw us practice spiritual principles in our life and it made him want to do the same. And people ask us all the time how we do it and we share with them the spiritual principles we learn from the program that we take into our home and we live by example.

23. What advice would you offer others in learning to love one another?

The first thing I would tell someone is you first have to find self-love and self-forgiveness. Because you cannot give something to someone else that you do not hold for yourself. Everything starts with you and ends with you. Do not look for someone to complete you or to fulfill you, but look to your partner to share with you, your journey and their journey. Look to inspire one another to live your dreams. Don't try and fix the other. Give them the freedom to live and learn. When you leave room to grow, your love grows with you both.

24. Write a 1 or 2 page narrative describing your relationship or describe your relationship in 10 words or less.

Looking back on my relations of the past and reflecting on where I am today in my relationship, all my life I had picked abusive relationships, whether it was physical, mental, or spiritual abuse, I have experienced it all. But working the steps and staying clean has given me a different perspective. I see where I was also the abuser—not just to others, but mostly to myself. I have learned that we attract what we are. But I was living in so much fear that it was easier for me to blame instead of taking responsibility for my life. I lived in a lot of fear of being alone. So I settled. But once I started to do the work, I was able to let go of some of those fears, and I no longer live in fear of being alone. I love me today, so it is not acceptable for someone to be in my life who does not *respect me. I have been blessed to have a man in my life that has done a lot of work and is open-minded still and lives a spiritual life. We allow each other the freedom to be who we want to be. I love sharing who I truly am with my husband because he never downs me or tells me that my dreams are stupid. We inspire one another to be all that we desire to be, no matter how far away it may seem, we can dream. And we can share our fears, even though my husband sometimes has trouble expressing what is going on with him, he see that there is work to be done. We know we are not perfect by far, but we are willing to do the work to reach wherever we are trying to go at the time. Respect is a big principle that we live by—and honesty, willingness. I know I have faults, but my husband does not beat me up with them. He loves me in spite of them. One thing I know is I cannot expect any more in my relationship than I am willing to give. I create my own unmanageability, which in turn spills into my relationship. If I continue to do the work on me, then I create a better relationship.*

Yes, I am married but that for me does not mean I own my husband. If he decides he is not happy in our journey, he is free to go and be with whomever or wherever he wants. I do not believe that we have to wait for a divorce or whatever the laws say. For me, our marriage is a commitment to one another not a chain. If that commitment no longer exists, then we are free to live our lives the moment we come to that decision. I brought this up because I have friends going through a break up and I see all the pain and hurt it is causing to many people. I honor my husband for as long as we are together, but if a time comes and our hearts are not with one another, I pray I have the strength to let go, and by doing that I feel I would honor the love we shared more. And I believe by living this way keeps our love stronger because we have freedom. I do not feel stuck here. I am here because I want to be, not because on August 25th 2007 we said, "I do." This is really were my heart is. And today we are still very much in love with each other. I do the work to love myself, so in return I am able to love him. I try not to focus on what he is doing and only concern myself with what I am doing. We lead by example in our home. We show each what we are doing. We don't tell each other what the other needs to do. And it works for us. My husband is the best man I have ever been in a relationship with. I have found the true meaning of the word relationship, and it is not ownership. For me to be in a relationship means I have someone I can share love with. I had it all backwards before. Today I am on the path of unconditional love. That is some DEEP LOVE! I apply the principles from the 12 steps and that have led me to other avenues that help teach me to be all that GOD create me to be. ONE WITH ALL. NAMASTE MEANS THE GOD IN ME RECOGNIZES AND HONORS THE GOD IN YOU.

OUR VOWS
Here is the promise I made to my husband on our wedding day.

My promise to you:

Long ago I had a dream to share my life with some one that was kind and caring, who would treat me like a lady, who would share in my dreams, someone who would love all of me, including my children who are a part of me, as well. Today I will marry that man. Today my dream has come true and this is my promise to you.

You have always inspired me to be all that I am and all that I want to be. I promise to do the same for you. I promise to practice the principles of giving and receiving. I promise to listen, to forgive, to trust, to communicate, to have respect. I give these so that I may receive them. I promise to open *my heart and my mind to your dreams and your desire, but without forgetting my own. I promise to always work on self so that I can share my true self with you. I know because we are free to be all that we desire, our love will live on forever. Today we honor the love we have created within ourselves to share with one another. For I cannot give what I don't have. I promise to always love me, and in loving me, I can truly love you without condition and without judgment. I know these principles are the true principles of unconditional love and that is my promise to you. I love you, Paul.*

Roger and Joan

1. A *brief* Bio (*age, sex, clean time etc.*)

Sixty three years of age, male, black, born in Philadelphia, PA. I have been clean for 30 years.

2. Describe family origin.

My father and mother were from Tennessee. My mother was only sixteen when she had me. I am the second of eight children; I have six sisters and one brother. My father was uneducated and could not read nor write. My mother had an 8th grade education—at that time was like college.

3. List issues you would describe as dysfunctional.

Everything was a secret. Talk was in code, which we all figured out over time. Nothing was ever explained in detail. You were asked to do something, even if you had never done it before, you were expected to know how it went. Beating, slapping, pushing—things we did to each other we thought were normal.

4. How did/do you feel about your upbringing?

I thought my upbringing was bullshit. Meaning having five sisters to compete with for everything, being poor and realizing that we were poor. On the other hand, I thought my upbringing was okay, having five sisters to take care of all the house work, cooking, cleaning, etc. Having women in the house all the time made it very interesting.

5. Were/are there any issues that have made relationships difficult for you?

One of the main issues is that I have been used to being catered to by women. All my life my mother and sisters always looked out for Roger. So, subconsciously, I still look for others to take care of my needs. I have gotten better because of the steps and traditions, the principles from them. I had been so accustomed to people taking care of me without asking, sometimes I think they should be able to read my mind. I think it and you do it (all in my mind, bad for relationships).

6. How did you resolve them, or, how do you live with them if still unresolved?

Having the desire to be able to take care of myself. I have been able to attract people in my life that care enough about me to allow me to take care of myself. They are healthy enough within themselves that I am left with having to take care of myself. Sometimes my little boy comes out and I feel myself getting resentful, but then I am able to think about my situation and realize how selfish I am being.

7. How would you describe an intimate, loving, nurturing relationship (utopian and real)?

Intimate relationship to me is letting others see what I am feeling and thinking at any given time. However this is an area where I still need a lot of work. I find it very difficult letting people in to my innermost feelings and thinking. I understand if I were to open up in this area, my life would take on a brand new meaning for me. Loving means to allow people in my life to be who and what they are, loving means to me to not judge them, just accept them, honor them, respect them.

8. How many times have you been married or in significant (long term) relationship?

I have been married four times. The first time was when I was twenty one, she was sixteen and pregnant, and her family thought it was the right thing to do. I was not in love with her. I didn't want to go to jail, and I did like the idea of having sex available. The second time, the woman was putting pressure on me, and so I married her without even being divorced from the first. (I was in active addiction.) The third was after taking care of the wages of the first two, and it lasted for almost fifteen years. My fourth is the one I am in now. I think the mistakes I've made in the other marriages have given me a lot of experience about what is expected in a healthy marriage and how to maintain it. I treat my wife the way I want to be treated.

9. What did you learn about yourself and about relationships from these experiences?

I've learned that I can only receive what I am willing to give. I've also learned that I can't give what I don't have. I've learned that if I want respect I need to give it. I've learned that sometimes I need to do things I don't want to do just because my partner wants to do them. I learned that I can be real selfish and I don't like the way it feels, and how it makes my partner feel. I like myself more when I am in harmony with my partner. I've learned that if I communicate with my partner, I can do just about anything that makes me happy.

10. How long are you currently married?

We have been married for almost a year. We have been together four years.

11. What do you believe are the most important things in maintaining an intimate, loving, nurturing relationship?

Trust. Not being a prisoner to the relationship. Having the freedom to express myself and have my own identity. Freedom to grow through my shortcomings. Having the support of my partner. Being open to my partner's view points even if it hurts my feelings. Being able to say NO without feeling guilty.

12. What struggles have you overcome?

Control. I realize that when I am trying to control that I am truly out of control. I want my partner to be a better housekeeper, to pick up after herself, to keep the house clean at all times, but it's just not going to happen. So I have made a decision to let it go. I'd rather be happy with my wife and have peace within. Every now and then when I am going through something I have the tendency to focus on things from the past, such as poor housekeeping or dishes in the sink to keep me from the real issues. ME

13. How do you live with each other's defects of character?

This one is easy. Every time I see her character defects I see my own. Sometimes I am able to smile, other times when I am in a bad neighborhood in my head, I react, but my reaction is only short-lived, because I see me. We are able to talk about them, sometimes we have a solution and sometimes we don't. I can't believe with awareness of others' character defects how I am able to see my own so clearly. Even when I am in denial about my character defects, I have someone to point them out to me. Men, this is what we talk about when we say acceptance is the key.

14. How do you handle conflict?

The easiest way for me to handle conflict is to handle it. I hate conflict so I try to keep it at a minimum. However, there *are times when conflict comes about and I think that I've been wronged, I will confront with a vengeance and most times in this situation, I come to realize that once again it was my thinking that caused this situation to get out of control. So what I am saying is that I need to always check my perspective on any given situation.*

15. What are the strengths of your relationship?

The strengths are recognizing that we are our own individual persons. And that we are different in the way we do things. To recognize my way is not necessarily the only way to do something. Listening to each other's concerns. Allowing ourselves to be silly around each other, to laugh with and at each other.

16. How do you create private time in your relationship?

Ask for it.

17. What are your happiest times together?

When we plan a trip or time together. When we are both hot for each other sexually. When we are grateful for each other. When we pray together. When we accomplish something together. When we support each other and acknowledge our love for each other.

18. How do you maintain romance and desire?

We touch each other on a regular basis. We kiss and hold each other. We have enough sex that it is special each time. I try new things if I am asked to, and sometimes if not asked. We acknowledge special days in each other life, birthday, anniversaries, etc.

19. What spiritual beliefs does each individual in the relationship hold?

I believe that what comes around goes around. I believe that the God of my understanding and I are one. I believe that there is no separation, that there is only one of us. One God, one universe, one of us. We share the same belief.

20. What are your common spiritual beliefs?

When we were able to buy a home together. When we were able to create a place for our children to come to and feel safe.

21. What would you describe as fruits of your relationship?

We believe that we create our own world. That life happens through us, not to us.

22. How does your relationship share with others?

We open our home, our hearts, and share our beliefs with other.

23. What advice would you offer others in learning to love one another?

First let me start by saying that my relationship was built on a spiritual connection with my higher power. Let me explain. After getting into so many relationships that didn't work or didn't last, it was suggested that I pray on the thing that I was looking for in a relationship. Once that was done and I had an idea of what I was looking for, I could record them on paper. This made sense to me, because I had been getting into relationships without even having a clue of what I really wanted. My list consisted of 12 things that I viewed as important in a relationship. They were:

- *Trust. For me the most important part of a relationship is trust, no matter what kind of relationship it is, if you are lied to by a spouse, parent, child, or friend, it breaks down the relationship and it hurts. Trust is number one on my list.*
- *Respect and understanding. I think that if I have respect and trust in what a person does, then I will be able to*

understand them more.

- Freedom (not controlling). Non-judgmental, not critical. Someone willing to work with me, not against me.
- A person that has other people in their life, other than myself.
- Great attitude about life, and one that is grateful.
- Affection. My wife lets me know that she wants to be with me, her smile brings sunshine into my day.
- Real sexuality. What I am talking about is not explicit sex. I am talking about a gut feeling that bypasses the mind and body parts and stimulates all the senses.
- Not keeping score. I understand one of the most dangerous and insidious activities that can creep into a relationship is the habit of keeping score. When love was getting started, in the beginning, my wife could do no wrong. It was easy to overlook the little things that were annoying. But little by little, as we get to know each other, expectations, both spoken and unspoken, begin to form. These are the times when I need to ask myself, "How important is it"? These are the times when I need to communicate more.
- Happy. This is one of the most enjoyable things about my relationship. My partner has showed me how to be happy.
- Working on self. The ability to work on self regardless of what is happening around us. Not forgetting that we have a loving higher power who is there for us. Inviting our God into our home and into our relationship.
- Last but not least, honesty. I feel free to be honest with my partner. This has helped us to maintain freedom in the relationship. Honest communication is the key.

Alice and Mark

This was not something I could sit down and quickly answer. I hope the information is still timely in view of your deadlines. In any event, I think this was a helpful overview for me, and am grateful for the opportunity to participate.

1. A *brief* Bio (*age, sex, clean time etc.*)

I am a 57 year old female, celebrated 22 years of sobriety 5/19/08, raised Jewish, now more of a Buddhist Jew.

2. Describe *family origin.*

Father (workaholic-alcoholic), mother (prescription drugs-diet pills, barbs, chronic obesity, passive), brother 5 years older (been a lifer on methadone program since 1969), identical twin sister (eating disorder, no drug or alcohol use).

3. List issues *you would describe as dysfunctional.*

I don't know how to answer—dysfunctional now? My pattern of eating—wanting to eat whatever I want and be thin. Addiction to sugar, flour and wheat. I prefer denial in this area. Dysfunctional in childhood? Dissociated to avoid the abuse, developed addiction as a coping skill as soon as I could.

4. How did /do you feel about your upbringing?

Upbringing…hmmmm…at least I didn't die, and the program offered me a way to grow up and heal. I was molested by my brother from age 9 through 12. My mother knew but didn't do anything. If my mother told my father, my father would have killed my brother, so no one told anyone. Essentially, I was sacrificed due to my mother's codependency and fear.

5. Were/are there any issues that have made relationships difficult for you?

I used to pick the bad boys, the sooner out of prison the better. I used to pick (and I still watch out for this) women who are dependent and weak (like my mother).

6. How did you resolve them, or, how do you live with them if still unresolved?

Resolved through NA, therapy (individual and group), treatment for alcohol issues, lots of support, and through God without whom I wouldn't have had the ability to put it all together. Still work on women issues…being attracted to needy women (mother) and dependent women (sister). I'm careful when I start sponsorship relationships…I avoid newcomers due to their neediness and my over-response to it.

7. How would you describe an intimate, loving, nurturing relationship (utopian and real)?

Respect, support, non-judgmental, fun, light, real. An example: Husband (Mark) doesn't put the dishes in the dishwasher. I asked him if he thinks they are going to fly in or walk in by themselves. He says no…he forgot again. I say, "oh," and he says, "Well…it doesn't make me a bad person." And I say, "No, it doesn't." End of issue. Non-judgmental. Accepting of each other's process. This would have (and did) occur with humor and love in our tone. In my book this is utopian and real in my life.

8. How many times have you been married or in significant (long term) relationship?

I had a "starter" marriage for 9 months at age 20. I was divorced for 9 years, and then married Mark. We've been married 28 years. One relationship in between was sex-addiction. That partner died in a car accident. All other relationships during the time between my marriages were either sex or drug based.

9. What did you learn about yourself and about relationships from these experiences?

10. How long are you currently married?

28 wonderful years.

11. What do you believe are the most important things in maintaining an intimate, loving, nurturing relationship?

Humor and spiritual principles. Open-mindedness: my way is my truth but not necessarily THE truth or my husband's truth, and not necessarily the only truth. Most often, I look at me and he looks at him. That gives each of us the power to change since that's the only power we have...the ability to change ourselves. Acceptance for each other's process... just because it doesn't look like mine doesn't mean it's bad or wrong. Integrity about owning feelings. Ability to have the ego-strength to stand up for what I believe and the ego-strength to acknowledge I made a mistake. Same for my husband. We are, essentially, ok and healing as individuals... this allowed our marriage to practically heal by itself.

12. What struggles have you overcome?

Overcome: I'm a non-practicing addict. I no longer live in self-loathing. I no longer feel worse than everyone else. I no longer obsess about hiding and what people think about me.

I don't live in my own projections of what I think and make up that people are thinking, or why they are acting the way they are. I love in the present and am ok just as I am. I am connected to my Higher Power in a way that offers comfort. I seek no more than I already have.

13. How do you live with each other's defects of character?

Not a problem…as we each work on our own, the impact has been greatly reduced or eliminated completely. Respect for each other's process and acceptance of it is probably the biggest key here.

14. How do you handle conflict?

Conflict is handled the same way. We talk. We acknowledge other ways to do it. Why we both think and feel the way we do. There is no need for anyone to win. There is no ego in our arguments. Each of us can get in the dog house…we let each other know when it's happening. Sometimes, we say, "You are backing into the doghouse," and that opens the door to what's happening. Also, when feelings are hurt, we get to tell the other what we need to have happen so we can let go of the hurt. For my part, it's been a card with something written in it. On his part, it's been a special recipe I don't often make. The question, though, has been integral in the letting go and moving on process.

15. What are the strengths of your relationship?

See above.

16. How do you create private time in your relationship?

We each have our own telephone line in the house. We used to wait to use the phone, so it was either him on the phone, then me on the phone, and then before you knew it bedtime. This way, we both do our calls during roughly the same time and we both don't talk after 9:00pm. Saturday nights are our night for socializing, and Sundays are always for us... never golf, or shopping, or single type activities. Almost always, couple stuff. The phone thing mentioned in this answer was huge here.

17. What are your happiest times together?

We have had such happy times. We have a screened-in patio and have nights outside with the dogs and music on. We like to lie on the same sofa with our feet in each other's laps. We like to go to the ocean together. We are in contact when apart and know what each other is doing. We never hang up without an "I love you." We bought a house when we were two years clean and then our recent home 19 years later. It was exciting and fun and incredible to see who we are/were and how it happened. There is love in all our exchanges. I can't pick out the happiest time...it's all good.

18. How do you maintain romance and desire?

We have great humor about Viagra. Mark is 65. About ten years ago, when Viagra came out, I was telling my friends how "dependable" it made Mark. We laugh and they laugh but it was a good thing for both of us. We now have Viagra dates. I'm responsible for the refills of the medication. We plan ahead. Mark has no ego about any of this. Neither do I. Also, sexual intimacy seems to have shifted from our aging bodies to a spiritual connection, and sex involves a lot of eye contact and kissing.

19. What spiritual beliefs does each individual in the relationship hold?

We both have a higher power unique to our individual needs. We're both Jewish but hold a lot of "first do no harm" beliefs. I meditate...he doesn't. He naps, I don't. It all seems to work.

20. What are your common spiritual beliefs?

Common spiritual belief is in the process of NA *and the program. It works if you show up. It works if you go to meetings. It works if you first do no harm. It works if you do the steps. There is a higher power for each of us as well as for the relationship.*

21. What would you describe as fruits of your relationship?

We are secure in our relationship to have friends of the opposite sex. A woman could flash her boobs at Mark and do a "come hither" (I'm dating myself here!) and Mark would look at her like she's crazy. Same for me. That security is wonderful. It allows me to do volunteer work that takes me away from home for 7 day stretches. It allows him to go on golf trips without a wife at home fretting. We are able to be there and give back to family, friends, and community and to NA. Our life together is the fruit of our work.

22. How does your relationship share with others?

Don't understand the question

23. What advice would you offer others in learning to love one another?

See above. I pretty much describe our relationship in the answer to every question.

Advice: *If each partner heals themselves and evolves, then the relationship heals and evolves like magic. Don't point the finger…look within. Find humor. Know that, unlike what we were taught, most things are not good or bad…they are "what is." Give up ego and know that most everything has nothing to do with you…the other person in the relationship has his/her own process. Accept the other's process with love and humor. Know that the ego isn't real and isn't necessary and let it go…learn to be real. Recover.*

Jeff and Barb

1. A *brief* Bio (*age, sex, clean time etc.*)

Male, 50, 20 years clean, married for 17 years with mother of children, 18m, 16f

2. Describe family origin.

Hillbilly, German/Scottish

3. List issues you would describe as dysfunctional.

Negative sense of self creates a whole lot of dysfunctional problems: feeling less than, emotional unavailability, intimacy issues, addiction.

4. How did you/do you feel about your upbringing?

I got some mixed messages about my folks and growing up. My folks did what they could do for me. Today I know about change.

5. Were/are there any issues that have made relationships difficult for you?

The negative sense of self that creates all the other craziness in my life.

6. How did you resolve them, or, how do you live with them if still unresolved?

By learning to love myself, I've found that I'm whole, complete, and not living that lie that there is something wrong with me.

7. How would you describe an intimate, loving, nurturing relationship (utopian and real)?

Just being in the room with [her] adds to my energy and moves my spirit. The tone of our voices. Eyes share a common thought or a look of encouragement. Sharing dreams, making time for each other, relaxing together, exploring our innermost feelings. Utopian, for real. Making ends meet financially and physically, getting the kids through school.

8. How many times have you been married or in significant (long term) relationship?

I've been married for 17 years, first marriage.

9. What did you learn about yourself and about relationships from these experiences?

I've learned that people grow apart, interests change along with how they feel about each other and what is important to them. When the pain of being together is greater than being apart we will change.

10. How long are you currently married?

17 years, a long time and its getting [lonely]

11. What do you believe are the most important things in maintaining an intimate, loving, nurturing relationship?

Having common interests, being able to meet each other's needs: spiritually, mentally

12. What struggles have you overcome?

Death, depression, kids, money, emotionally crippled, one in recovery, one not

13. How do you live with each other's defects of character?

Loving caring manner, by being spiritually accountable for our own well being.

14. How do you handle conflict?

Not well. With a group conscience and different points of view. We just do what's best for us in the end.

15. What are the strengths of your relationship?

We are both rocks—hard to move without reason. One sees black the other white. Totally opposite each other except when it comes to the kids.

16. How do you create private time in your relationship?

We don't much anymore.

17. What are your happiest times together?

Traveling and sharing new experiences.

18. How do you maintain romance and desire?

Romance and desire have faded from her having depression.

19. What spiritual beliefs does each individual in the relationship hold?

Her beliefs have been in question since her mother's death eight years ago. I believe there is a power that we can all tap into for strength to relight the ember of our soul to stoke a full fire inside.

20. What are your common spiritual beliefs?

There is something greater than us: love.

21. What would you describe as fruits of your relationship?

Our son and daughter.

22. How does your relationship share with others?

We are rarely together to share with others.

23. What advice would you offer others in learning to love one another?

Be happy and seize the day in a loving way.

24. Write a 1 to 2 page narrative describing your relationship or describe your relationship in 10 words or less.

When the pain is great enough there will be change.

Lisa and George

1. A *brief* Bio (*age, sex, clean time etc.*)

Born February 26, 1951, in Gettysburg, PA
57 *years old, female*
19 *years clean and sober*

2. Describe family of origin

I came from a happy, mostly functional, family. My mother and father are married 60 years. I have one brother and one sister. My mom stayed home to raise us kids. My mother was an only child. Her biological father (alcoholic) left when she was very young. My mother was raised by her mother who was a very independent, hardworking, progressive woman for her era. She met and married my step-grandfather while working in Washington, DC. She found and purchased a home in Northwest DC. She and Grandpa and renovated the home. She then found a farm in Gettysburg which had no plumbing. They traveled up on weekends and made the old brownstone house a home. The farm had 50 acres which they farmed.

3. List issues you would describe as dysfunctional (within your family of origin).

My father had 5 brothers. They lived in Gettysburg on farms. Grandma H gardened to provide food for the boys. She baked bread and pies twice a week! She raised chickens, pigs, and cows. They butchered and ate all of them. I remember her cutting off the chicken's heads, and they really did run around! My father went into the Navy in 1944. He flew in a Navy plane that spied on Russian ships at sea and kept the US safe from attack. He was a self-employed building contractor.

My sister is the best older sister ever. She excels at anything she does. She is my rock. She went to school and majored in psychology, got her masters, and minored in art. She made art her life. She taught art for a year and is an accomplished mosaic, ceramic artist. She travels all over the country to do public art.

My brother worked with my father for years. He married after dropping out of school. He had 2 children, divorced; remarried, had 2 step children, divorced; remarried, no new children. His 2 biological children were passed between their mother and my parents.

We were a close family growing up. I was rebellious, always getting in trouble.

Shame and guilt-based discipline. Lack of communication about sex, relationships, and feelings.

4. How did you/do you feel about your upbringing?

I feel I was given good morals and values. Good work ethics and honesty were important. I was the baby, somewhat spoiled by dad but disciplined by my mother. We were raised in the Lutheran faith, attended church and took catechism. I have good parents, they did as they were taught.

5. Were/are there any issues that have made relationships difficult for you?

In the past I was fearful of losing a relationship so I ended *them before he could. I had been rejected in high school and chastised by my old boyfriend and his new girlfriend. This rejection was very disheartening and hard for me to understand. My fear kept me from making a commitment to one person, so I played the field for many years—of course, during my active addiction. No one could be trusted, so I couldn't make a commitment. There was a definite issue with trust.*

6. How did you resolve them, or, how do you live with them if still unresolved?

Time away from relationships helped me. I was once again getting close to a man and found out he was unfaithful. I fought to try and keep him, but after embarrassing myself, I moved on. I was resolved not to get into a relationship and to just party with my girl friends.

The girl I lived with met a guy who had a roommate. We went to play pool at their place, and that is where I met my husband. But at the time I wanted nothing to do with him, I wasn't going to let the same thing happen again. He was sweet, kind, persuasive, outgoing—not like me, quiet and shy! He was fun and kept after me to go out. I gave in and the relationship kept growing.

7. How would you describe an intimate, loving, nurturing relationship (utopian and real)?

Rare. My relationship with my husband was sometimes loving, sometimes nurturing, but not all the time. We developed a habit of being there for each other and a kind of close understanding of what each needed. It was almost an unspoken connection that developed over time and being together. I knew when he needed my attention, so he could tell me what he was feeling.

We knew the unconditional connection of not fearing being

abandoned, lied to, or cheated on. (There were plenty of times the disease reared up and self-centeredness took over. I want what I want!)

I stood up for my husband and he for me. He was very protective and expressed it when he felt I was being attacked or misrepresented. He was very committed to me. We always said I love you to each other everyday and were affectionate.

8. How many times have you been married or in significant (long term) relationship?

Once.

9. What did you learn about yourself and about relationships from these experiences?

It's give and take, compromise at times. I wanted a life-time commitment. I was determined to get married and stay married. I don't take commitment lightly.

10. How long are you currently married?

26 years

11. What do you believe are the most important things in maintaining an intimate, loving, nurturing relationship?

Honesty, open-mindedness, and willingness. To keep learning, trying new things together that maybe interest your partner but not you, and vice versa.

Communication is very important. Don't expect your partner to know what you want—tell them. They aren't mind-readers.

12. What struggles have you overcome?

Putting expectations on my partner. I learned to take care of myself and not to impose my standards but express my feelings about, say, chores, the yard, the garden. I would *compromise on how I thought things should be—life is too short to care about a perfectly clean house or perfectly mowed lawn. My priorities changed. I learned not to engage in differences in areas that don't really matter.*

13. How do you live with each other's defects of character?

I work on mine, he works on his. God takes care of me—I pray for His will for me and the power to carry it out.

I can't expect him to be anyone more than the best he is today. I learned to accept him as he is and know he loves me.

14. How do you handle conflict?

Usually we argue about stupid stuff. How to hang wallpaper or not hearing each other when we talk. A few choice nicknames and pet names come to mind. Never did we bring up the past or say hurtful, shameful things that leave permanent scars. And we didn't stay mad, we said what's up and moved on.

15. What are the strengths of your relationship?

Reliability, being committed, love, independence.

16. How do you create private time in your relationship?

We used to set a date, say next Wednesday night, to stay home and don't answer the phone, etc.

17. What are your happiest times together?

We really enjoyed going on trips and exploring new things. We traveled the world and tried scuba, snorkeling, went to concerts, camping, good restaurants.

18. How do you maintain romance and desire?

We would go on dates for dinner, tease each other, say romantic things. George use to tap me on the shoulder over and over and say "Guess what? Guess what"? and I kept saying "What? What? What?"! Then he would kiss me and say, "I love you."

19. What spiritual beliefs does each individual in the relationship hold?

Trust, faith, love, and hope.

20. What are your common spiritual beliefs?

Trust, faith, love, and hope.

21. What would you describe as fruits of your relationship?

A true understanding of commitment and trust. Definitely our long-term friends and recovery we've gained as a result of our commitment to each other and the program.

22. How does your relationship share with others?

I believe others can see the trust we have for each other. They see us as a unit and as individuals, staying clean, having fun, helping others. Being a good role model of a couple staying clean and carrying the message, and that it works if you keep the focus on yourself and not try to change the other.

23. What advice would you offer others in learning to love one another?

Don't try to change each other. You can't. Acceptance is the only way. Don't put too many expectations on each other—there are some definite ones like coming home, calling home, being reliable, but remember you can't change anyone but yourself.

Compromise, give and take.

Have fun—try new things together!

Be open-minded and willing.

LISA AND GEORGE

Kiss everyday and tell each other that you love them.

Be loving and kind. Be positive and supportive.

Let go of control—surrender is the key!

Marriage is a life-time commitment not to be taken lightly. It is truly a gift to find someone to love and to spend your life with.

I was very blessed to have had such a loving and giving man in my life. I am truly blessed and grateful for the last 27 years. God has given me more than I should have had in the short time George and I had together.

Don't put off till tomorrow what you can to today. Tomorrow many not come.

Glossary

Alcoholics Anonymous describes themselves as a nonprofit fellowship or society of men and women for whom alcohol had become a major problem. Their primary purpose is to stay sober and help other alcoholics to achieve sobriety. www.aa.org

Narcotics Anonymous describes themselves as a nonprofit fellowship or society of men and women for whom drugs had become a major problem. They are recovering addicts who meet regularly to help each other stay clean. www.na.org

12 Steps – A path towards spiritual awakening practiced by AA/NA Members.

12 Traditions – Principles practiced by members of AA/NA to find the love of God in the decision making process and direct the behavior of members with each other and their respective fellowship as a whole and the community in general.

Autonomy – The privilege of self determination and individual or group identity.

Inventory – A process for calling ones behavior, attitude and moral character into question.

Sponsor – Someone with whom we develop a confidential and loving relationship for the purpose of receiving or giving guidance and direction in the application of the principles found in the 12 Steps and 12 Traditions in our lives, so that we may find freedom from our addiction and learn to live a new way of life.

Recommended Readings

Alcoholics Anonymous – 4th Edition

12 and 12 – Alcoholics Anonymous

The Basic Test of Narcotics Anonymous – 6th Edition

It Works – How & Why, Narcotics Anonymous

The Holy Bible or your chosen book of spiritual insight

Reflection on the Art of Living, A Joseph Campbell Companion, Diane K. Osbon

Song of the Bird, Anthony DeMello SJ

With Open Hands, Henri J.M. Nouwen

Life Lessons, Elisabeth Kubler-Ross and David Kessler

On Death and Dying, Elisabeth Kubler-Ross

Celebration of Discipline – Revised Edition, Richard J. Foster

If the Buddha Dated, Charlotte Kasl, Ph.D.

Narcotics Anonymous Pamphlet – The Triangle of Self Obsession

Your warmth has offered me passage through many
a cold night. Awakening I see your face illuminated
by the morning sun to be captured in my mind's image
and brought forth many times in the quiet moments
of the day. You are an inescapable part of my being;
you are my sweet, sweet heart.

– by RMck for SMck